S___

AND

HEARD

Stop Feeling Lifeless, Shake Free
of the Unseen Forces Holding You Back,
and Live Your Life in the Now

SEEN

AND

HEARD

Stop Feeling Lifeless, Shake Free
of the Unseen Forces Holding You Back,
and Live Your Life in the Now

LESA PETERSON

 Torchflame Books

Seen and Heard: Stop Feeling Lifeless, Shake Free of the Unseen Forces Holding You Back, and Live Your Life in the Now

Lesa Peterson
https://lesapeterson.com
lesa@lesapeterson.com

Published 2023, by Torchflame Books
www.torchflamebooks.com

Paperback ISBN: 9781611535198
E-book ISBN: 9781611535204
Library of Congress Control Number: 2023910107

Grampy,

You always answered my thousands of questions
and encouraged me to just be me.

I feel the warmth of your smile,
proud of the woman I have become.

I love you.

CONTENTS

CONTENTS

INTRODUCTION

A s I walk into the five-star restaurant, beauty surrounds me. I see all the tables covered with white linen, fresh flowers, and candlelight that seems to dance to the rhythm of the sea. The hostess greets me and walks me to my table. As I'm seated by the window, I look out at the setting sun, the sky lit with color. I smell the beautiful hint of the cool, salty sea as a soft breeze caresses my face. The scene before me is captivating. Voices from the next table pull me back into the restaurant. A young couple is being seated. They are telling the hostess they are on their honeymoon.

My mind seizes up. I have come to Santa Barbara from Las Vegas to see a well-known therapist so I can find out what's wrong with me. I desperately need to know why my husband is having a second affair. Am I crazy for forgiving? Is there something so unlovable about me? I need to know what I did wrong, why I am never enough, and why I don't measure up. I am doing everything I can to be good enough, to be worthy of his love, but nothing seems to matter. I've been a good wife, doing all the things I should, but I always seem to fall short of his expectations. I feel like a loser, but I am hopeful that tomorrow this therapist can give me some relief from all the pain and tell me what's wrong with me.

I hear my server's voice. He is announcing my food, a filet mignon, baked potato, and roasted asparagus. I have never felt so alone as I sit amid this beauty and look out over the ocean. I know my husband is with this woman. The pain of knowing that grips my body, and tears roll down my cheeks. I struggle to eat between the tears. Is this the end of my marriage? What's wrong with me? I never wanted anyone to see my pain, and here it is, happening in public.

The newlywed woman from the next table gets up to go to the ladies' room. Our eyes meet for a moment, and I smile as if to reassure her I'm fine. I don't want them to see a broken-down, middle-aged woman dining alone, her energy drained and health declining. I feel so lifeless. All I taste of my wonderful meal is the salt of my tears and the pain of being alone.

I must keep up the appearance of being fine and hide behind a smile, but I know deep down that I can't maintain that facade of perfection any longer. More tears roll down my face as I see my life fading in the sunset before me. I am like a piece of driftwood taken out with the tide, never to be seen again. My server brings a few tissues to me and touches my shoulder for a moment in silence, as I sit alone in this beautiful place, listening to the rhythm of the ocean, and wonder what I have become.

I feel angry at life. I want to scream: Why? Why me? Why did the love of my life have to die when we were so young, so long ago? Why am I here? Why am I being punished? I am desperately seeking answers. How can I be on the brink of losing a second marriage? I am a good and loving wife. My husband shouldn't be cheating on me. Yet somehow, I am being punished for not being good enough. I don't know what I'm doing wrong. I feel empty, like my world has stopped. It's a familiar feeling from so many years ago when I got word that my first husband had died. The pain of doubt creeps in, and sorrow takes over as I am reminded about the tragic way I lost him. The hurt on top of hurt is too much to bear...

I can see now that the woman who sat in that restaurant on that day, her marriage a shambles, was a woman who had not yet found what she was looking for. Once before, when I'd faced tragedy in my life, the unexpected death of my first husband, I had turned to yoga. It had been my first stop, my entry into an unknown world. I remember as I moved on my mat, following the instructor, I started feeling like I wanted to cry. I thought, "wait—what's going on?" I made it through the class and even though I was embarrassed, I talked to the instructor about my experience. She told me that this happened a lot in class as we move and connect to our bodies. Even though I didn't know exactly what was going on, this was the first time in a long time I felt connected to my body and the emotions stored in it. I kept searching and I found energy work, a mind-body therapy that addresses healing on the physical, emotional, mental, and spiritual level. After that day, I dove into Reiki, a Japanese healing method, medical qigong, the traditional medicine practiced in China, and sound therapy, using vibrational sound waves on the body to promote well-being. I could feel the movement of my body and in my body. I could feel space opening up. As I began to open space in my body, I also opened space in my mind. I started to understand the connection of the body and mind. I saw how they spoke to one another. I started to see the unseen forces that surrounded me like air, moving me about my life. I saw the control these forces had over me.

I Am Afraid to Be Seen

I have always felt like I can walk into a room, and no one will even notice I am there. I can't remember ever being seen or ever being enough. I don't want to be the person out front, but I will do all the work making them look good. I have had many jobs where I was the right-hand man to the CEO. All the staff would come to me for direction, and the customers would ask me for help, but when it came time to make a presentation, I always deferred to the CEO.

Am I afraid to be seen?

I feel like people won't like me once they get to know me. I'm not very smart. I don't want anyone to know that I'm so dumb that I can't tie my shoes, as my kindergarten teacher told me. I'm not very pretty, either. All my friends had boyfriends when I didn't. All these voices are echoing in the recesses of my mind. Are these the reasons I fear being seen?

One day, in separate chance encounters, I had four different people tell me, "I see you and I have seen you." I was really taken aback, to the point of being triggered. One of the encounters actually caused me to go into a fight-or-flight response. I could feel the energy in my body racing. I noticed it and thought, "What is going on with me?" but I kept moving on with my day. It wasn't until later that day I had time to start questioning it more, but I really couldn't figure it out.

Each day, under the blanket of the stars, during my early morning walking meditation, I always listen for the messages of the universe. Each morning's walk connects me to the universe, but more importantly to myself: my body, mind, and spirit. As I start walking and I listen, I hear many things. This morning was no exception and what a profound message I received. As I walked, I asked the universe, "What do I need to know for today?" The answer came clear as a bell and instantly: "Lesa, you equate being seen with trouble." I said to myself, wait—what? Why would I believe that? Again, the answer came clearly and instantaneous: "It's about your conception." My conception? I thought for a moment and then it all came flooding in.

My mother was fifteen when she got pregnant with me, and my biological father was twenty. They had been dating for about a year. In the early '60s, much shame and judgment came to a woman who got pregnant outside of marriage, let alone a girl of fifteen. Out of fear, my mother chose to hide my conception from everyone but her cousin for three months. She hid me under her clothes for as long as she could, but eventually, she had to tell my father and her parents. My father chose to leave, her parents were disappointed, and my mother had to quit school to take care of me.

Because our body stores our experiences, I believe that during that first trimester, I felt that need to be hidden so there wouldn't be trouble. My mother's fear of her pregnancy being exposed and getting in trouble for it became my fear. All my life, I have unknowingly equated being seen as trouble, something to avoid at all costs.

Let me pause my story with you and share. That word "unknowingly" pointed me to more questions. Once I realized that a force had been acting on my life—and I didn't know it—I started to look for other places in my life where this might be happening. I started noticing it in other people's life stories. I felt like I was onto something, a much bigger question. What other unseen forces have been holding us back?

In the stories of my husband's affair and my conception, I could sense a common thread. For the first time, I started to see what was shaping me. I started to see a big unseen force that was directing my life, the social constructs. The social constructs are the fabric of life that all life is built upon.

In this introduction, I'll give you a taste of the major unseen forces that are shaping your life. As we move further into each chapter, we'll go deeper into each of those unseen forces. I'll give you an in-depth look at how they are impacting your life, and I'll help you understand how you can shake free of the forces and live a better life now.

Do as You're Told

Social constructs are all around us. These are constructs like religion, family, marriage, education, and employment, just to name a few. We rarely question them because we see them as pillars of our society. They are the very fabric of our being and for most of these, there is no changing them. We feel like they are set in stone and are for the good of all. We don't think these constructions have ever changed. We forget that they have and some of the changes have been big ones, like the earth is flat, or that the earth is the center of creation and the sun and the planets rotated around it. Then there are social constructs like African-Americans being slaves and women being the property of men that most don't even think were social constructs—just really bad ideas.

Religion as a social construct has really deep roots, as it constructs our eternity. If we aren't in the "right" religion, we may be going to hell for all time. There are so many religions that it divides us and leaves us feeling anxious and uncertain at times. Even within our own religious beliefs, there are "rules" that must be followed to be good enough to get to wherever we are going for eternity, which leaves us feeling never enough because we broke a rule that God made.

In recent years, sweeping changes have come to family and marriage constructs. It has been a long-held belief that only a man and a woman should be married and build a family. This construct had to be challenged all the way up to the U.S. Supreme Court. It is these ideas of virtue or vice, right or wrong, good or bad, that hold us captive. We have been fooled into believing that things are black and white. If you are good, then you do these things, and if you are bad, then you do these things—it simply is not true. Once a yoga instructor told me we really should be seeking balance, but at the time I really didn't get it. Now it has become clearer. We have no idea what balance looks like nor do we really even want it. We desperately need to be good, right, and enough, and we have a "value menu" to measure ourselves against what has been constructed for us. We just have no idea that it has been constructed——"it's just what you do," most of us think. We don't even stop to think that not all of us are meant to get married and have children. I know, that seems really crazy to say, but one size does not fit all. The social construct leads us to believe that there is something wrong with us if we are alone.

Higher education is one social construct that leads us to think we are smarter than those without it, leading us to believe we are better. While most of us would never say that out loud, it is our belief. A higher educational degree leads us to a better-paying job that in turn gives us more value. All these thoughts are on a subconscious level, but they impact us on a real level. No one wants to accept that they think that someone else is less-than because they don't have something we do. We may not believe we think that way, but I think we can agree that if we don't have that education, we feel less than someone else. We are always wanting something more to make us feel better about ourselves. We end up living by mottos such as, "Somewhere else is always better" and "More is all I'll ever need."

The social construct around employment is a soul-crusher. The jobs we do can quickly become who we are and how we determine our value. There are constructs around what jobs a man should do and what jobs a woman should do. Looking at the medical field, the construct is that men are the doctors and women are the nurses. That has changed some, but for the most part, it still holds true. This leaves women feeling like they are less than men. Money also contributes to value in the employment construct. The more money one makes, the more valuable they are in our constructs. This is an area that is so misunderstood. We are not all meant to be doctors or lawyers, but we can be pushed into a "good paying" job by our parents, and other sacred people around us.

As social constructs are the fabric of life, what is valued within them becomes a thread to our value, our worth in life, as we have been constructed to get our value from outside of ourselves.

Value by Design

I believe that we all have gifts to share with the world and if we can really cultivate those gifts, we will be fulfilled and have the means to support ourselves. We just never really have the opportunity to search for where our gift lies.

For some of us, our gifts are very apparent, but for others, we need to uncover them. It is in our childhood that we should be seeking our gift with the help of an adult, but most of us never really get the opportunity.

Our parents think they are preparing us for life by focusing on our getting good grades to get the job that pays the most. Yet, when we are not doing what we were meant to do, our souls suffer. The need to be enough, to be good, keeps us lifeless. If we could just see that our gift was ditch digging, we would be fulfilled and taken care of by digging ditches. When we love what we are doing, it makes others want to do it, participate in it, watch it, buy it. We rarely get to see someone doing what they love, but we feel it when we see it.

All these constructs are external sources from which we derive our value. When we believe our self-worth comes from outside of us, we can only fail. Identifying and understanding all these unseen forces gives us a way to discern how these forces work together to keep us lifeless and how to live a better life now.

When we get our value and worth from outside of ourselves we can only feel like there is something wrong with us when we don't measure up. We look at others and start judging ourselves against what they have... Why am I not married? Why don't I own a home? After all, we believe that social constructs and their values are the only way to happiness. This leaves us with false and limiting beliefs about ourselves because we aren't all and don't have all the things the social constructs tell us we should be and should have.

Wait—What?

Our limiting beliefs are another area that holds us back and leaves us lifeless. Some of the more common limiting beliefs are:

- Bad things always happen to me.
- You must work very hard to have money.
- I could never start my own business.
- I am not lovable.
- I am not good at speaking to people.
- No one will listen to me or care about what I have to say.
- I'm not smart enough.
- I will always be alone.

All of these beliefs start as thoughts we have told ourselves. Over time they have become beliefs. We just need to stop and question them—Is this really true?—then understand how that belief has been holding us back from our true potential. Then, we can shift into that new belief that will actually propel us forward to the life we want to lead.

We don't feel good about ourselves because we have been fooled into believing that our value comes from an external source. Those limiting beliefs that form cause us to develop a sense of self that is flawed. Because those external sources can be taken away, we can never measure up, which causes us emotional strife. To alleviate it, we defend ourselves. This defense is known as the Drama Triangle.

The Trio of Trigger

The Drama Triangle keeps us in a perpetual cycle of dysfunctional social interactions. The triangle is a power struggle between the roles of Victim, Persecutor, and Rescuer. The Victim belittles oneself with the attitude of "I can't do that on my own." The Persecutor belittles others' worth with the attitude of "It's all your fault," and the Rescuer belittles others' skills with the attitude of "Let me help you. You can't do that on your own."

We are in one of those three roles in every relationship and interaction unless we know about them. When we are in these roles, they take on a life of their own; we get something from them that makes us think we need them. These roles keep us distracted from the bigger picture of the social construct that is running in the background. When we blame, feel responsible for others, or just feel helpless, we end up in a fight, flight, or flee situation.

It is so easy to find ourselves in the Drama Triangle when we haven't experienced our own power through finding our true selves. We end up playing the game by someone else's rules because we are listening to their voices as if they are our own.

Shouting at Midnight

The voices we have playing in our minds are mostly critical voices from past experiences and they are not even our own voices—they just seem that way. We have had these voices playing in the background for so long that they are part of our operating system. We listen to them as though they always tell us the truth, but they rarely do. These voices come from many places—our parents, teachers, family, and friends. We listen to them because it's what we have heard for so long that we start believing it—

it must be true. These voices tell us all kinds of lies...You will never get a good job... You will never get married... You will always be overweight...

We listen to these voices because we live in a dominator culture that is based on fear. We unconsciously scan the horizon for the next threat. Unfortunately, a coworker or our spouse can look like a threat to us.

Frozen

Most of us would like to think that we interact in the world out of our strengths, but most of our time is spent acting out of our fears and insecurities. We don't even really think about it because it has become such a habit and we have people around us who "fit." We don't keep people around us who are a constant threat to us.

Women in particular have been taught that we are the weaker sex and need to be protected. We are taught to never go anywhere alone as we might be attacked. While it's good to be aware of our surroundings, we need not be placed in that mindset of fear when we are alone. I believe that this is the reason that when women are out shopping or to lunch, they tend to go in pairs. Have you ever seen two men get up from the table and go to the bathroom together? Not often, but women frequently do. That is a fear that has been placed in us and we don't even see anymore. It has become a "just what you do." We don't even think about why.

Because we live in a dominator culture where someone is on the top and someone on the bottom, we are always looking for the next threat on the horizon. It causes us to live in fear, with our bodies running full of adrenaline and cortisol, ready to fight or flee.

Our bodies were not made to be in fight or flight for that length of time, and we unknowingly are in that state for most of our day. We can't keep up with that amount of heightened awareness throughout the day. It's not a wonder that 43 percent of Americans are overweight. If we don't use cortisol, it gets stored in our bodies as fat.

Our bodies are constantly sending us messages, but over the years, we have been taught to not listen to them anymore. We have become a culture so disconnected from our bodies that when our health suffers, we look to drugs or surgery to cure what ails us.

The Truth Center

The key to unlocking our vision is our connection to our bodies. Our bodies hold our life stories and are giving us signals all day about ourselves and our environment but we either ignore or medicate those signals. We soothe with food, drugs, sex, gambling, alcohol, TV—we'll try anything to alleviate the pain. That pain in your back is trying to tell you something. Listen. Sit with it. It has a voice and wants to give you information. By the time pain is involved, we haven't been listening for a while. Pain is our body's only way to communicate with us, to force us to pay attention. Even then, we don't really stop. We just think we must endure the pain. As we slow down and reconnect to our bodies, we create space for that body-mind connection. That is the key to being seen and heard, seeing and hearing ourselves, then taking that into the world.

The Resurrection

Take a moment here to reflect on what brought you here. What nudged you to pick this book off the shelf? Was it that you have never felt seen or heard as a woman? Or was it never feeling good enough, but you had to keep up with the look of perfection? Maybe you weren't really fulfilled by the promise of wife and mother but were too afraid to pursue your dream. Whatever brought you to this point, I'm right here with you.

As you begin to identify the ways in which you have been moved by these unseen forces of the social constructs, external self-worth, limiting beliefs, the drama triangle, your voices, fears, insecurities, and the disconnection from your body, you will feel like your world is falling apart, and it is. The illusions that have been built will start to unravel. Some will feel like freedom and some will feel like death.

I have been where you are, searching for something that I couldn't fully understand or even see. I will walk with you during those dark times of introspection and reassure you during those lonely times of separation from beliefs that you held dear. I will help you sift through the rubble left behind and reconstruct a life full of love. I promise color will come back into your life, clarity will return to your mind, and the flow of energy will return to your body. Your job is just to trust the process, breathe, and take one step at a time.

CHAPTER 1

SHHHHH!

Finally, it's my turn to say what I want to be when I grow up. I'm a sophomore in high school, and I tell the school counselor I want to be an apprentice in the trade program. There is silence, so I say, "You know, the electrical, plumbing, construction program."

As the counselor starts to speak, I feel sick to my stomach. "Lesa, you know that program is for boys," he says. "You can't do that kind of work. We have a cosmetology program for you, or you can follow the secretarial program." I am furious but I don't have an advocate with a big enough voice. I think that's not fair, and why is that? What is wrong with being a girl?

Fast forward to my junior year, and Air Force recruiters visit the school. I'm ready! I want to be a fighter pilot. I'm so excited as I listen to the presentation. Afterward, when I go to speak with him about being a pilot, his words crush me. "I'm sorry young lady, but girls can't be fighter pilots." Not again! My mind flashes back to two years ago, when I heard, "That program is only for boys." I'm starting to feel a pattern being set in me, although I don't know it. It's the pattern of women being less than men.

It's the summer just after I graduated from high school, and I'm sitting in the church pew watching my best friend get married. I feel the warm kiss of the summer breeze brush across my body as I'm thinking what's wrong with me? Why doesn't anyone love me? This is the second close female friend of mine to get married. I think, *I'm going to be an old maid so I better figure out how to take care of myself because*—and here come the voices that reign in my head again—*You know no one wants you. You know you didn't have boyfriends in high school like everyone else. You are just a loser.* The voices died down and I sat alone with them until they were quiet. They may just be voices in my head, but clearly I wasn't fitting into the pattern of what my life should look like.

Fast forward twenty years. The phone rings and a voice says, "Where are you?" To the voice on the line, I think, *you called my house, so obviously, I'm home.* "Why aren't you coming to the door then?" the voice said. I was outside in the backyard, I reply. Suddenly a tenderness takes over the voice as it says, "Just come to the door." An unsettling sensation overtakes my body as I answer the door and see a man from the police department. I don't know him. I only know he is standing there with my husband's police partner and his wife, and the sheriff and his wife. They all looked so serious.

The one I didn't know says, "Lesa, I'm sorry to inform you that your husband has been killed in a training accident." My mind froze for a moment. Then, it raced. How could this be? What happened? How can I be alone? How can I survive on my own, I'm going to be homeless... *No*, the voices that were stronger than my own thoughts said, *you can have the renters move and you can move back into your old house. You might be able to swing that, maybe.*

Oh, you just got your income tax refund so that will help with his burial and funeral, so you should be okay. Then one of the people on my porch says, "Lesa, let's go inside." I open the door wider and turn back into the house with all five of them following me to the living room. Now I am a woman who doesn't have a husband.

What We Do to Be Valued

Naturally, I felt sad and shocked that my dear husband had suddenly died. What I wasn't prepared for was how quick I was to judge myself—tell myself that I was nearly worthless now that I didn't have a husband. Why was I so quickly feeling worthless because I was no longer a wife? How did I learn to think this way? The social constructs are ideas we have created and agreed upon as a society. These constructs have become the very fabric of our lives, and we don't even see them any longer. They have become like the air we breathe, an unseen force that keeps us alive. In our society, we each have an idea of what we are supposed to be doing and what ought to come next. Those expectations are handed to us, and we don't think twice about them because it's just what we do.

You want to fit in and be valued, right? You want that so much that you don't even notice the messages you have taken in and then acted as if you agreed with them. Pink is for girls; blue is for boys. Big boys don't cry, and little girls should be seen and not heard. Women are the weaker sex and men are to be the providers and protectors. You are too young to know anything. You're too old, what do you know?

These are all social constructs that we live by every day. We don't even realize just how they are impacting us in our daily lives as they have become so normalized. We take them as always being set in stone. We have long forgotten that they were made up and we made them. We have been fooled into believing that they were made by some authority who knows better and has our best interest in mind.

Our culture has made up all the social constructs but some of them seem more valuable than others. They have become the cornerstone of our culture, while some fall away at certain ages. Think of the associations you have for the colors pink and blue. In recent years, it's become a fad for expecting couples to have a gender reveal party. The focal point of the party is something like a cake cutting, balloon release, or some sort of smoke bomb in which blue or pink is revealed. They don't have to tell us the gender—when we see blue, we know it's a boy; when we see pink, we know it's a girl. We live our lives without thinking or questioning a lot of things; we just take them as how it is supposed to be.

Another thing we don't question is the pattern of our lives. The pattern for most of us is that we go to school, and graduate from high school. Some of us then go on to higher education while others get a job; next is marriage and children. It's just what you do, most would say. I didn't want to have children when I got married. Mostly because I am the oldest of five, and my siblings were my children. I was quite a bit older than they were, so I got a dose of the responsibility children can be, and I wanted no part of it. I know you all say it's different when they are your own and that may be true, but I know plenty of women who are divorced and wish they didn't have children since they now have to care for them alone. I hear a lot of women saying I wish I would have known I had a choice.

How old were you when you found out there was no Santa Claus? Who told you? How did it make you feel? Important adults are the ones who tell us these stories and I can't help but think about what it does to a child when they find out the truth. Santa Claus, the Easter Bunny, and the Tooth Fairy are some of those social constructs that fall away at a certain age, but they are social constructs just like having to get married, get a good job, and an education. Some of these social constructs that we learn in childhood as myths are seemingly innocuous, but they are the beginning of the programming we are to follow. By the time we are old enough for those big programmings, like marriage and family, we have been following along without much questioning for such a long time that they are deeply embedded. Because we get so much of our worth from them, we don't even see them as anything but normal. They become just what you do to fit in. I know what you are saying: what I am supposed to do, then? There is nothing wrong with those things, most of us will take that path yet it will look very different for each us.

I loved music growing up. I started playing drums in fourth grade. I loved the marching band. I was the only girl in the drum section, and I was the tallest and strongest for a few years until the boys caught up with me, but I didn't get to carry the big bass drum when we marched or even the snare. I carried a tenor drum. Yep, I bet you have never even heard of that kind of drum. When we practiced inside, I rarely played the drums. I played the other percussion instruments like the tambourine, chimes, cymbals, and triangle. None of the boys wanted to play them so I had to, at the order of the band director.

In my freshman year of high school there wasn't a marching band, so I opted for choir. I loved singing and I got to sing every day. As much as I loved music, you would have thought that I would have done something with music or in the music industry, but that was not to be. I lived in a rural, agricultural area, and given my family and their background, a music career would never be an option for me. The social construct for me was to get married and have children, then if need be, I would get a job, most likely in a factory. If I was lucky, I would marry a farmer.

The social construct requires that women have a provider-protector for themselves and their children—we would call that a husband. This is where the constructs start going awry. We don't see these unseen forces for what they are. If we don't look like everyone else, then there is something wrong with us. We see ourselves, and others, as failures and losers when we don't have those things that everyone else seems to have and be enjoying. These forces actually limit our beliefs, keep us disconnected from our bodies, and disguise themselves as a promise to a happy life, but they really hold us back.

These patterns are set for us because we are bombarded with them at a very young age. Fairytales like Cinderella and Snow White unknowingly leave little girls with the idea that being a wife and mother is what should come next in life. If they don't achieve that status, then there must be something wrong with them, not something inherently wrong with the system. We are very impressionable and programable as young children because our analytical minds are not fully developed. These are important times for our well-being.

An Impressionable Age

Growing up, I lived in the country, where there were no streetlights. It was dark at night, but you could still make out things once your eyes adjusted. I was about eight years old when one night, I noticed bats flying around outside, so I told my uncle and dad. To get me to go back to bed, they told me that if I didn't get into bed, the bats would fly through my window and bite my neck. From that night on, I was afraid of the dark and I had to sleep with the covers pulled up around my neck. That comment at that time made its way into my mind and body, as it isn't until around thirteen years of age that our analytical mind is developed. We think we are an advanced society, but we forget that at one time, we thought the world was flat and that the earth was the center of our solar system. I know there are things we believe right now that all those scientists and scholars are telling us, that are not true. We believe them because they told us they are right, and we aren't really supposed to question them. Still to this day, I have to sleep with the covers pulled up around my neck even though I know those bats aren't going to bite me.

Just as our minds store memories of the past, so do our bodies. Have you ever heard a song that takes you back to a time and place? When I hear, "You Dropped the Bomb on Me" by the Gap Band, I immediately feel the skates on my feet and the breeze on my face as I am whizzing around the roller rink. I feel an excitement in my body—it's palpable, I can even smell the popcorn and hot dogs at the concession stand. It's been almost forty years since those days, but the body's hold onto memories is powerful.

We have stored all the things that have happened to us in our bodies and minds. They work in concert to help us in life, but for the most part, we have shut them off due to social constructs. Anything that the social constructs have deemed as irrelevant or invaluable to our lives, we don't pay much attention to. Oh, don't get me wrong, we connect to our bodies in an egotistical way of judgment and value, but not in the natural way of life. In our culture, most women are expected to have that 36-24-36 figure to be valuable. We don't realize how much that is controlling our lives. Most women would say that it doesn't account for much in their lives, but there is no way that it doesn't. It's like the air or gravity; Just because we don't see it, doesn't mean that it's not there. It affects us every day of our lives until we understand how. It's like Socrates said, "The unexamined life is not worth living."

Our bodies hold the events in our lives. We may have no conscious awareness of this until we hit those times when the storehouse starts getting full. We have lost that mind-body connection, and it is killing us. We are becoming more obese, depressed, and suicidal. We are finding ourselves at odds with others more frequently, and everything seems life-or-death. We keep moving faster to get away from the feelings, but the only way to regain ourselves is to stop and listen. We must look within. This is something we are not taught and most of us simply don't have the tools for it.

We have been taught to look outside ourselves for the fix. If we can slow down and listen to our bodies and mind, we have the answers. Someone needs to help us start on that path and give us tools for that journey. Just as we need to exercise our physical bodies, our energetic bodies need attention as well. We are all energy aware; we just don't know it, as it has lost its value in our culture. When we meet a person and just click, that's energy. When you get that gut feeling about something, that's energy. It's there to guide us, but we have been disconnected from it for so long that we have forgotten about it and how important it really is.

Eastern philosophies of medicine approach healing in a more integrated way. Traditional Chinese medicine is based on the principle that the mind and body are intricately entwined. We hold emotions in our bodies; anger is stored in the liver, fear in the kidneys, sadness in the lungs, worry in the spleen, and joy in the heart. We rarely recognize any of this because we have become so disconnected from our bodies. If we are still and listen, that mind-body connection tells us many things. We just need to reconnect to ourselves to hear it, but we don't see the value in it, so we tend not to do it. We don't realize how much we stop the flow of our energy in our bodies with our thoughts. Simple things like holding our breath or stuffing down emotions lead to energy being stuck in our bodies. We need to be conscious of it so we can start to open up those places again. Pain in our bodies is blocked energy, a signal that we need to stop and take notice. We can make it worse or better, depending on our focus. If I have a headache and I tell myself that I'm the kind of person who always gets headaches just like my mother did, my head is going to continue to hurt. As we become aware of the patterns and stories we are telling ourselves that are not true, we naturally change course to a higher understanding and direction in life. The mind is so powerful; I believe that we can heal ourselves if we can get out of our own way. We just don't know how much disbelief we have in our lives, how much we believe things can't happen. We really have to get the mind-body connection going before we can do that. If we take the time to uncover those unseen forces that are guiding and controlling us, we can interact in the world in a completely different way and get different results.

We need to identify those social constructs and really take a look at how we feel and what we believe about them. We don't question ourselves enough. We need to identify where we have stored all those events in our minds and our bodies and rework them to understand them and clear them out. You will be really surprised at what you think and believe. I recently had a sexual experience with a younger man that triggered so many things that I had no idea were in me or that I was believing. I was fine during the experience, but the next morning I was extremely unsettled. I was so focused on what he was thinking that I lost sight of myself. I was worried and stressed out about it all. I felt like I had ruined a friendship at the expense of my ego because it felt nice to be wanted. But more than that, it gave me worth in our social construct. In our culture, women are programmed to need a protector-provider. That is why we need a man on a subconscious level. Our value comes through the external source of being a wife and mother.

While I felt wanted and attractive, I knew that this relationship wasn't going to bring that provider-protector to me. So now I have just devalued myself in the marketplace. I am worth less than donkeys and blankets and have just become more of a burden to my family. I felt like I was a bad girl because I instigated the experience- I kissed him first. I have been told if you start something, you have to finish it. Don't be a tease. I don't think I was necessarily looking to have sex. I just wanted the boost from being wanted and he was young and attractive. It's actually crazy all the things that came up from that experience. When you give yourself the space to think differently and feel the energy in your body, you will be amazed at what you find. You might find, in that sad tension across your chest, that you love to be the center of attention; you've only been in the background because you didn't want to get punished again by your parents for making a mistake. You may recognize you reach for food anytime you feel that knot in your stomach because food is your source of connection to people. When you are alone you overeat because you feel unwanted. We can learn so much by listening to these physical symptoms we often shrug off.

In What Do You Place Your Worth?

We don't have the opportunity to explore ourselves enough when we are children. Our culture believes that children need to be protected and guided, but what happens is we stifle our children. Our fears and insecurities become theirs. We don't mean to do it; it just happens. We are unconsciously measuring ourselves, judging ourselves, against an unseen construct that hinders us. The social constructs have assigned a value to everything and we want the most valuable things in our lives so that we belong and feel good about ourselves. We wholeheartedly believe in those assigned values and seek them at all costs. What we don't understand is that not everyone is meant to be a doctor, attorney, professional athlete, or politician. We think we want those things because they have so much value in our culture.

We continually look outside ourselves to what we can find in our lives that give us our worth. Do I have the right car? Do I have the newest iPhone? Do I have a "good" job? All of these are just things or roles that we have tied to our worth. They feel very real to us, but these are the things that keep us lifeless. When we are being whom we were made to be, all those external things become meaningless and fall away. We just don't really get the chance to explore ourselves, to try things on. Somehow, we are expected to know and do, but it's really someone else's know and do. We get moved about without any real input ourselves as to what is next. We think we do, but think about it: what did you do after high school? What real options did you feel you had? This should be a time for us to explore, but we are pressured to move to the next phase of our lives, for some higher education, a job, or marriage. How is an eighteen-year-old supposed to really know what she wants to do without exploration? This is really the first time she may have the sense of making decisions for herself, even if the social construct only gives her a few options. We feel the pressure of those authorities telling us not to make a mistake or it will cost you your future.

I can tell you from experience that exploration as an adult looks and feels ugly. It feels so wrong but it's necessary. It's the only way through to uncovering those unseen forces, seeing your limiting beliefs, and reconnecting to your body. It will feel uncomfortable, and at times lonely, but that's when you know you're making progress. You have to do things differently to see the patterns that you learned and work them out.

At age thirty-three, I began to explore myself after my first husband's unexpected death. He was a police officer assigned to the search and rescue team. While he and another team member were doing ice climbing training, there was an avalanche, and he was killed. It sent me reeling. It was the first time as an adult that I was alone. I started to question who I was and what I wanted in my life, which was something that I had never done before. I didn't know how big the world was and how many choices I actually had. It started with little things like doing yoga and signing up for classes in dream interpretation. I started traveling more, changed jobs, and became more adventurous. If something came to my mind, I tried it. I was in enough pain that I didn't care what others thought about me. I did what felt right to me for the very first time in my life. I know people were concerned about me because I didn't act in a responsible, reliable way. I wasn't that quiet, reserved person that always did for others before herself. I became someone unfamiliar to them and it frightened them. I know some thought I had really lost it. To some, my actions led them to believe I was in denial of Russ's death and just running from it. I wasn't acting as a widow should, as if there is such a thing.

In my journey after Russ's death, I discovered a world that I had never seen before. I accessed a part of myself that I had never known. Because I was in so much pain, I looked for ways to deal with it. I didn't want to lose my connection with Russ so I started talking to him as if he was still with me. As I did, I felt his presence in a more profound way. I felt an energetic connection with him on a level that I had never known before.

The pain was so raw for me that I was energetically open on a whole new level. I had always been told that I was an emotional person. Little did I know that I was a highly intuitive, sensitive person. We all have instinct and intuition; we have just cut ourselves off from them.

To access it, we must feel into ourselves. Going within is not something we are used to doing when we have a problem. We have been taught to look outside of ourselves for answers. Our answers can only come from within when we feel connected to ourselves, our breath, our bodies—it's when we get still and listen that the answers come.

In the beginning, this is the way we have to work through everything: through great pain. The good news is that once you start seeing those unseen forces and uncovering your patterns, it does get easier. You will build a toolbox of resources that you will use to work through these unseen forces. You will start seeing all those layers of forces that have been shaping your life, those forces that limit your beliefs and keep you disconnected from your body. This is a path of no return. Once you start down it, you won't want to go back because you can see the cost in your life. As you experience life returning to you, as you see the forces that have been holding you back, you will step center stage of your life with excitement as you are living a better life now.

See it, Hear it, Live it

Let's reconnect by noticing our breath.

Take a moment to get comfortable, close your eyes, and bring your awareness to your breath. Notice the breath coming in, and the breath going out. Follow the breath with your awareness... follow the breath all the way in... and follow the breath all the way out... Don't try to change it in any way. Just breathe in and breathe out. Breathing in, feel the breath as it passes through your nose... breathing out, feel the breath as it leaves your nose. Keeping your awareness lightly and gently on your breath...

With each inhale, I am breathing in...

With each exhale, I am breathing out...

When thoughts come in, as they always do, acknowledge them without judgment, and let them go. Let them drift away like clouds floating through the sky, and bring your awareness back to your breath.

With each inhale, I am breathing in...

With each exhale, I am breathing out...

Each time your attention moves away from your breath, distracted by a thought, physical discomfort, or maybe something you are worrying about or a concern you have, notice the thought, acknowledge the thought, and then consciously let it go. See it as if you are letting go of a balloon that floats away, and bring your awareness back to your breath. Breathing in and breathing out, notice the rhythm of your breath.

With each inhale, breathe in peace and stillness...

With each exhale, let go of any concerns...

When you bring your awareness to your breath, you are connecting your mind and body. This connection will help you create space, which will allow your energy to expand. It allows you to see things from a new perspective.

Continue to breathe in this way for as long as you like, following the breath all the way in, and following the breath all the way out.

As you bring the mediation to an end, keep your eyes closed for a moment and notice how you are feeling, your body and your mind. Take a moment and offer yourself gratitude for taking time for yourself to be quiet and bring yourself back into balance.

Slowly come back into the room, aware of your body. When you are ready, open your eyes.

CHAPTER 2

WHAT YOU WANT

I can feel the cold rising up from the medical exam table. As I'm lying there feeling vulnerable and exposed, he begins his exam. The silence is broken by his voice. I hear the doctor ask, "When was your last pregnancy?"

It's not my usual doctor, so I indulge the question, saying, "I've never been pregnant

"Interesting," he responds. He looks and feels around some more, as I start to panic. It feels so uncomfortable as he presses harder and deeper into my body. With what he said next, I would have fallen over if I had not already been lying down. "Well then, we should do a pregnancy test. It looks like you're pregnant."

I can't be pregnant. I'm on birth control. *Oh my god, what if I am!* I've heard horror stories of all the things that can go wrong with the pregnancy and the baby if you get pregnant while you're on birth control. My husband and I have talked about having children, but we aren't sure that we want children. At least not right now.

As I sit in the empty, lifeless exam room, I'm scared and worried, sitting alone for what seemed like forever, awaiting the results. The doctor comes back in and the look on his face is alarming. "You're not pregnant" he says, "but there is something going on."

I'm thinking, "Something. What something?" He says that I need to go to a specialist. Wait... what is happening?

So, the next week, I go to the specialist for another exam and more tests. The specialist believes it's just a uterine fibroid, but he wants to do some more tests to rule out cancer. Oh my god, cancer. This week is the longest week of my life. Finally, I'm back in the specialist's office. He gets right to the point and tells me the fibroid is not cancerous. What a relief!

Three months later at my scheduled checkup, I can see concern move over the doctor's face. Now what?! The doctor finishes the pelvic exam and ultrasound and asks me to come to his office after I get dressed. He has another matter to discuss with me. The fibroid has grown significantly in three months. He tells me that if I want to have children, it's now or never, as I will need to have a hysterectomy. He feels that I have six months to decide if I ever want to have a child. As the fibroid grows, it will become too big to allow me to carry a child to term.

I feel the life drain out of me. I don't want to make this decision right now—I'm only twenty-eight years old. This feels like an ultimatum. It's just not fair! I thought I had plenty of time to make this big decision. I leave the doctor's office crying, but somehow, I arrive home, although I don't remember the drive. I walk into the house and see my husband is home. I start crying as I walk over to him and hold him. He asks me what happened, and I tell him what the doctor discussed with me.

My husband and I have been married for eight years now and have discussed having children several times. We have always decided that we can wait—after all, we are still young. But now we must make a decision. I'm angry, worried, and scared, all at the same time. I'm angry that I don't have any more time and must make a decision right now. I'm worried that I'll make the wrong decision, and I'm scared to become a mother right now.

In the end, we decided not to have a child, but what an excruciating decision it was. I didn't realize it at the time, but it was among the first of many decisions that I would choose to go against the social norms. I had just chosen to diminish my value as a woman by taking away my ability to have a child. What would others think of me? People were already regularly asking me when I was going to have children. Was I less-than now?

Our Worth and the Social Construct

Remember from the previous chapter that the social constructs are a set of beliefs and ideas that we have shaped and agreed upon as a society. These constructs are all around us, and they move us about our day. These constructs have become our guidance system, and we have given them the power to determine our worth and our value. They influence our decisions without our ever knowing it.

Everything in our lives is socially constructed, and within that system, values are placed on each of the constructs, so some constructs have more value than others. Within the social construct of family, women are the nurturers, and they take care of the children, while men are the providers and heads of the family. While this is not how all families are constructed, it is the "best way" as defined by the social constructs. This is where all the values start adding and subtracting from your worth.

I never realized how much of my worth came from being a wife and mother. I started thinking about what else gives me worth: owning a home, having a job from which I can retire, working hard, always getting it right the first time, being thin, being smart and strong, having people always like me, making everyone happy, being the one everyone goes to for help... This is how we get sucked into the social construct. All these things are great, but they should not be tied to how we think about ourselves. Things come and go, and when your value is tied to them, your value comes and goes, too. That leaves you with an uneasy feeling, and now you're constantly trying not to lose, or trying to gain, things to feel good about yourself.

We are not all created to "be the best" in every social construct, but we have been fooled into believing that it is possible and that we should be. We are all not meant to be a doctor, attorney, or CEO, but we have given so much value to those constructs that we look past our gifts and strive for the money those jobs make. Money is a quick way to becoming important and valued in our culture, as the social constructs tell us the more we have, the better we are.

The value menu keeps us believing that someplace else is always better and that more is all we'll ever need. That list of values has been set up by the social constructs to keep us wanting, and this must be deconstructed. It is our intrinsic value that we should look to for guidance. Our worth should come from inside ourselves, not from something external that is arbitrary and can be taken away.

What do you attach to that gives you worth? Is it the role of wife and mother? A job? Education? While all those things are good, there is always someone better, more talented, or with more education. It's easy to see how that can leave you feeling less than others. To reduce the grip of the value menu in our lives, we need to think in a new way.

When we can feel that trigger inside ourselves, the one that makes us reach for our coping mechanism- food, alcohol, social media, etc.- then we can slow down and reprogram our worth. We can ask ourselves, what am I feeling? What value am I attaching to that feeling? Why is it making me feel this way? When we step back and are able to distance ourselves from that value menu, we can see ourselves from a different perspective. We are all "good enough" just as we are. There is nothing external that can add to or take away from our value.

Dominator Culture, Co-operative Culture

There are two different ways in which cultures or societies are organized: the Dominator style or the Co-operative/Partnership style. The Dominator style is constructed through a hierarchy of male-dominated power, where those at the top of the hierarchy use a set of beliefs to dominate those at the bottom. The Co-operative/Partnership style is built on reciprocal altruism, one of equality.

The Dominator style is an authoritarian construction based on fear and force, where a high degree of violence and abuse is socially accepted. These attributes of control and domination are the norms. They are desired and seen as moral. This construction leaves us with an inner critic that is judgmental and that finds fault in all we do. It leaves us feeling like we are never enough, and it makes us anxious about being good and doing things the right way. Nazi Germany and Stalinist Russia are extreme examples of societies built on the Dominator style.

In the Co-operative/Partnership style, there is no hierarchical control, so there is no built-in violence. This style is based on democracy and egalitarianism, where empowerment leads to higher levels of functioning. Empathy and non-violence are highly valued, creating an acceptance of our emotions and the ability to freely express them, which leads to a strong connection to our bodies. To find examples of the Co-operator/Partnership style of society, we need to look to the Inuit and the Bushmen. These cultures use the gifts of each individual toward the greater whole.

In our Western culture, we operate under a Dominator style construction. We are taught at an early age that someone is on top and someone is on the bottom, and at all costs, we must be the ones on top. Even when we get to the top, it's never enough, as we feel those clawing at our feet to take what we have worked so hard for. Now we fear losing it.

We learn early in childhood to obey orders without question and to carry a harsh voice in our head that tells us we're not good enough, we don't deserve love, and we need to be punished. Dominator cultures are based on control that is explicitly or implicitly backed up by guilt, fear, and force. It divides us into in-groups and out-groups, where those who are different from us are seen as enemies and must be destroyed or conquered.

You can see this happening all around the world—for example, in the war between Russia and Ukraine that begin in 2022. In basic terms, Ukraine wanted to grow and change, and in doing so, it became a threat to neighboring Russia.

This also happens in our interpersonal relationships. We don't realize it is happening because it has been set up by the social constructs. Think about the relationship between parents and children—parents have the power and direct their children. This seems like a good thing, protecting our children, but it can also be destructive as it can leave our children feeling like they never make a right or good decision in life.

This dynamic also appears in our social construct of marriage. For most of us when we get married, the man is head of the household. These unseen forces of men being the protector/provider leads to men having a dominant role, which can leave women struggling for control and feeling less than men. We want to believe that marriage is a partnership, a give and take, of the best that each has to offer, but we fail to recognize that hierarchy of the Dominator style that creeps in.

The social constructs have a chart of accounts and a ledger that we subconsciously record in every day to determine how worthy we are. We all have our gifts and talents to offer the world, but we have been deceived as to what they look like. When we use an external source for our worth, we can never be enough. That is how the social constructs keep a hold on our lives. We give our intrinsic value over to a power that we don't even see. We have spent so long being what someone else has decided is important and valued that we don't even know ourselves any longer.

For example, we look to those people in our culture who seem to have what the social constructs promise if we are good enough and do all the right things. We want to have the lives of the rich and famous. We look up to those people because their lives look fabulous to us. We think they don't have any problems; after all, they have everything that we are promised. They have looks, a great job, a beautiful wife or handsome husband, well-behaved children, a big house, fast cars, money, success, prestige, and power. This is the life we strive for and feel as if we are promised if we follow the plan of the social constructs.

The Obligations of the Social Construct

We all have expectations, duties, and obligations that we are not aware of in our relationships because of these values we have set up. They are the quickest path to destruction if we are not aware of them. Think for a moment about how you define mother. Or how do you answer, what is a good daughter? Or what makes a good employee? While we think most people share our thoughts and beliefs, they don't. We have similarities, but it's in the specifics where we can find the conflict.

Take a moment and think about what it means to you to make a birthday cake for a friend. What comes to your mind? Do you make one from scratch? Is it chocolate, white, strawberry? What kind of frosting is on it? Buttercream? Whipped cream? Do you add a filling? Maybe you just make one from a box mix and use frosting from a can, or maybe you order one from a bakery?

As you can see, there are so many birthday cake options, but you have one in mind that you aren't even aware of as being "right." This is where conflicts can arise, especially if they are tied to your value and have become "just what you do." Does being a good friend mean you know what their favorite cake is? Say that being a good friend means to you that you know what your friend's favorite cake is, and you make it from scratch for them. When they show up with a box mix of brownies for your birthday, you would feel slighted.

The value structure in the social constructs is very fluid, even when it looks like something more concrete. The social constructs change over time, but they always feel like they are set in stone without ever changing, so we never really see them influencing our lives. It wasn't until the 1848 Married Women's Property Act that women could own property, and only since the 19th Amendment in 1920 that women could vote. Women were not in the workforce. Their job was to care for their husbands and children. As women were seen as the weaker sex, and as property themselves, they were seen as incapable of having anything meaningful to offer to society, and certainly had no valuable opinion of their own.

These are social constructs that changed over time and ones that most of us take for granted. Women unknowingly still feel the effects that those times had on us. That leaves us with a lingering sense of being less than others and fear for our survival. I know it's not something we like to admit, but think about it for a moment. If we couldn't own property and couldn't vote, we would have no meaningful way of taking care of ourselves and we no voice to change anything.

As the social constructs are slowly changing, we are not. We have been conditioned to remain in the roles defined for us by the social constructs that are inherited from our parent's generation, but they are outdated. It can be difficult to accept or even see the new social constructs that are in play now.

In my mother's generation, men were the breadwinners and worked outside the home. Women generally didn't work outside the home but cared for the household and the children. For my generation, women started working outside the home, but those old ideals from the previous generation still held sway. Now, women aren't just caring for the household and the children, but they are working, usually full-time outside the home, but they are still expected to juggle both the work outside and inside the home. This dynamic leaves women overworked and stressed out because they can't keep up with all the expectations in their lives.

'It's Just What You Do'

We don't even see that we still hold onto these beliefs because we keep ourselves so busy and just do what we have always done. It becomes a just "is" or an "it's just what you do" kind of thing. We don't realize that we could do something different, even when it's not working for us. We have gotten into the pattern of rarely questioning things. Not questioning things holds us where we are.

These are how the values of the social constructs play out in our lives. They become our worth, something we will sell our souls for. These constructs have become the cornerstone on which we build our lives. We give little thought to a lot of things because it's just what you do... it's just what you need... it's just what you want...

After high school is the time when we should be discovering and searching for what we want our lives to look like, but all we find is a well-worn path to follow and we are expected to set out on that path. There is no self-discovery. We are wound up and sent out to marriage, children, and a job from which we will retire thirty or so years from now.

When we must follow the path in order to have value, it makes our lives less fulfilling. We know there is something missing, but we are always pointed in the wrong direction to find it, down further along the path.

The social constructs tell us that if we get off the path, we might get lost, hurt, or killed. Our fears set in, and we just settle. After all, it's what we have seen all of our lives and it's what someone important is telling us.

When someone tells us what to do and how to do it, or that we can't do something, we have the instinct to resist. This is called the opposition reflex. Opposition reflex causes us to push or pull against the forces that are pushing or pulling us. When we don't see the forces that are moving us, we are in constant opposition reflex without even knowing it. The struggle leaves us lifeless, on edge, and wondering what's wrong with us. Not having that time of discovery keeps us all longing for a connection to ourselves. We look in food, drugs, sex, alcohol, work—any place to get a little relief from the opposition.

Not Smart, Not Pretty

I have felt so dumb and weak all my life. I was never anything much in my mind. I'm not smart or pretty, so I never felt very valuable. I never got noticed in school. I felt like I always fell through the cracks. To this day, I feel like I can walk into a room and never be seen. I didn't seem to have any of the social constructs growing up that gave a little girl any worth. Now, I believe what I was feeling was a sense of worthlessness.

I love the quote from Maya Angelou, "You only are free when you realize you belong no place. You belong every place—no place at all. The price is high. The reward is great."

We are all unique individuals with special gifts that our world needs. We concede those gifts, never having fully developed them, for something that we are told is better and more valuable in life. I've heard it said that the number one regret of the dying is that they wish they would have had the courage to listen to the voice inside instead of letting everyone else dictate to them. There is nothing external that can really give us value, as it can be taken away. We are enough and worthy just by being. Our value must come from within ourselves; that can't be taken from us.

See it, Hear it, Live it

Let's connect by walking in nature. Let's take a walk around our neighborhood. Look at your neighborhood as if it is the very first time you have been there. Look with curiosity. Look at things as you would if you were on a vacation. Adventure a little. As we look at things from a different perspective, we get new insights and ideas. The wisdom that comes from these new insights is invaluable in our lives, and it directly leads to external changes.

When we use our senses, we are connecting our body and mind, and we are in the present moment. Most of us are just on autopilot. We are usually in the past or the future, but rarely in the moment. Have you ever driven home or to work and then not remembered the trip? You were thinking about how you were going to get the kids to soccer on time tonight, or what you needed to do once you got work? All this leads to the disconnection from ourselves. Our physical disconnection leads to our emotional disconnection. When we don't know ourselves, we tend to follow the well-worn path that others have set for us.

Before you start walking, let's take a moment to connect our body and mind. Close your eyes and slowly take in a deep breath, hold it for a moment, then slowly let it out. Do this for a few breaths, and then return to your normal breathing rhythm.

As you start walking, use your senses to notice the world around you. Listen for a moment. What do you hear? Your feet striking the ground as you walk? Your neighbor getting into their car? Birds chirping? Cars on the street? The wind? Just notice... what is your experience?

Now let's see if you can change your experience. Just be curious about what you heard. What did you think when you heard your neighbor getting into their car? Did you focus on your neighbors or their car, or maybe something totally different? Why? Do they always park their car on the street in front of your house and it bothers you? Did you think about how they are nice neighbors because they always bring the trashcan up from the curb for you? Does their car alarm go off frequently? We tend to have set patterns of thinking and don't realize there are many ways to see things.

Now, what do you see? Clouds in the sky? Cracks in the sidewalk? Your shadow on the ground? Trees blowing in the wind? Just notice your experience. Again, see if you can change your experience, using the same questioning process as before.

What do you feel? The sun on your face? The breeze against your hand? The temperature—does it feel hot or cold? Just notice your experience. Again, see if you can change your experience, using the same questioning process as before.

Finally, what do you smell? The ocean? Pine trees? Wood burning in a fireplace? Hot dogs on a barbecue grill? Just notice your experience. Again, see if you can change your experience, using the same questioning process as before.

Take a moment and think about what you have experienced. Were you able to change your perspective and see things in a different way? This is one way of finding yourself and identifying those social constructs that have been set up for you. Being able to create a little space for yourself gives you an opportunity to see more of those unseen forces that are holding you back.

CHAPTER 3

YOU CAN'T DO THAT

As I arrive at the residence, I see two marked patrol vehicles parked outside. I exit my vehicle, grab my camera and collection kit from the trunk, and slowly make my way to the open front door of the residence.

This is an older area of the city, and the houses are showing their age and disrepair. As I walk to the door, I notice all the neglected homes on the street. I see windows boarded with plywood, roofs with well-worn or missing shingles, broken-down cars in the driveways, and children's bicycles and toys abandoned in the front yards.

As I enter the home, all eyes turn toward me for a moment. I see a uniformed officer standing with his arms crossed in front of him. He has two adults handcuffed and seated on the couch. As I look at the couple, I notice the young woman's face is pale. Tears run down her cheeks as she cries softly. The young man slumps over with his head in his hands and stares at the floor. I see what appear to be drugs and drug paraphernalia on the coffee table in front of them.

I notice movement from across the room and see another uniformed officer seated at the kitchen table with two young children. Coloring books and crayons cover the table. The children talk quietly but are restless, as they are up and down from their seats exchanging crayons. It is eerily quiet in the house, yet the tension is palpable. There is a sense of despair in the air, and it's building with every passing moment.

I approach the first officer and he tells me that they are awaiting child protective services to remove the children from the parents' custody. As a crime scene investigator, usually, by the time I arrive on scene, the event has already happened. The officers have already dealt with the situation and I am just documenting the scene. But today everyone is still here. It is Father's Day, a day that is supposed to be filled with celebration, but this family is waiting to be torn apart.

I quickly get the information I need from the officer and start documenting the scene by taking photographs of the condition of the kitchen and living room. I can hardly breathe and have such a sick feeling in the pit of my stomach. I want to get out of that room. I go to the back of the house and find the children's bedroom. A single mattress is on the floor. There is a clothes basket on the floor with clean and dirty clothes mixed in; a few pairs of pants and a couple of shirts lie on the floor. There are a few puzzles scattered over the floor and a Jack-in-the-Box sits in the corner.

As I am taking photographs in the bedroom, the six-year-old appears, and he tells me that the officer told him to get some clothes for himself and his sister. I stop my photography and let him gather his things. As he is gathering the clothes, he starts to cry. He digs through the clothes basket and pulls out a wrinkled nightgown for his sister.

He turns to me with tears running down his cheeks, and says, "Please don't let them take me from my mommy." My heart breaks, as I kneel down and hold him for a moment. He holds on to me so tightly. Now tears start to run down my cheeks. "I'm scared," he says. "I know that my mom and dad do things that are bad, but I don't want them to go away."

"I'm sorry that you feel scared, it's okay to feel that way right now," I say.

Grabbing my face with both his hands, looking deeply into my eyes, he says, "I don't want to go with those other people. I just want to stay at my house until my mom and dad come back home."

Putting my hands over his, I softly say, "I know you don't want to go with those other people, but it's just for a little while, until your mom and dad come back. You and your sister can't stay here by yourself."

His brow wrinkles, "They won't be gone forever?"

I smile, "No, they won't be gone forever. They will be back soon."

As his back straightens up and color returns to his face, he says, "Okay, I'll go tell my mom and dad we will go with those people until they come back home."

As I leave the scene that day I think, *I can't do this anymore.* My soul is being torn from my body. It feels as if it's being ripped apart by wolves. It's been almost two years now since my husband's unexpected death and I'm starting to feel again. I'm conflicted, though. Crime scene investigation has been my dream job for so long. I worked three long years to get it. It's a really great job, it has good pay and benefits, and I can retire from this job. *Lesa, you're just being silly. Every day isn't going to be like this. Get a grip and move on.*

I know deep down that I've changed, and I will leave, but my limiting beliefs keep me there struggling with myself for another six months. I was taught that you should get a good job, work really hard, stay there for thirty years, and retire. It doesn't matter if you like the job or not; you just have to take care of yourself and be prepared for the worst-case scenario. Those same voices tell me if I were to leave that job, no other employer would want to hire me because now I'm a job hopper. I'm also getting older, close to forty, and no employer would want to hire an older worker, especially a woman. Those same voices ask, *who do you think you are anyway? You don't just get to leave a great job because you don't like it. Do you think you're someone special or something? You've changed. What are you talking about, a dream? Who dreams? Get back in line, and get back to work.*

These are all the thoughts, those limiting beliefs, I'm having because of my beliefs and values surrounding work. I don't realize that those beliefs and values aren't even really mine. They were given to me early on in my childhood by authority figures, my well-meaning parents, grandparents, teachers, and the social constructs. We are constantly getting messages from external sources that just slip in and become a belief or value without our even knowing it.

Some of these beliefs and values that have come from our parents and families can be some of the most damaging for us as they have been with us the longest. They have become very difficult to see because they are part of our fabric of life. They have become so normalized, and we no longer think about why we do these things. It's only when there is a conflict with someone that we have the opportunity to see them. It's in that split second before we react, before we enter the fight or flight response, that we have a moment to pause and ask, what am I feeling or what is happening. However, most of that time is spent defending ourselves and blaming the other person, or worse—beating ourselves up.

What's Holding You Back

These limiting beliefs come in all shapes and sizes. You would be surprised at some of the things you believe. Some of your limiting beliefs just sit on the surface and trip you up, while others are deep in your core and are rotting you from within. One of my limiting beliefs is perfection. If it's not perfect, then it's not good enough. I believe that for me to be good enough, I have to do it right, meaning perfect. Even if it's something I've never done or seen before, I'm expected to do it to perfection or I'm not enough. It is one of those beliefs that is at my core and has shaped my life for a very long time. It's been with me so long though that I didn't even see it anymore. It had caused me to lead a mediocre life, one that wasn't fulfilling and that was void of any real joy.

We rarely consider how we think about things and why we think the things we do. Once we become aware of our beliefs, we can work towards not letting them define our lives by bringing them into the light. How do they feel? What do we see? Is this really working for me?

We can start to question these beliefs from a child's perspective, one of fearless curiosity.

We just have to pull that one loose thread, and everything will start to unravel. Somehow, we have just settled, accepting that our life will never get any better. At times, there seem to be so many loose threads we don't dare pull one because we have enough going on already. We just can't stand one more thing going wrong. That's exactly when you need to pull a thread, any thread. Then stand back and really look at what you see.

We usually have to be in so much pain to make a move. I don't want you to be in that much pain to start the process. We can begin to think in different ways to get different results. We just need to identify how we are thinking and then why. It's then that we can change the direction of our lives.

Take a moment and think about how you see money. What is the first thing that comes to mind? Money is the root of all evil? A penny saved is a penny earned? I'll never be wealthy? Wealthy people are a**holes? I'm always broke? Money doesn't grow on trees? You will find that you have a lot of beliefs around money once you start really thinking about it. It might take some time to get to those limiting beliefs that are really holding you back because you are going to see them as "normal." We think this is the way everyone thinks about _____, so we don't need to question it.

When we start looking at our beliefs, we can see where we want to change them because we want different outcomes in our life. If we think that all wealthy people are a**holes, we aren't likely on a subconscious level, to want to have money because we want people to like us- we don't want to be that a**hole. If we believe that money doesn't grow on trees, we are living in a scarcity mentality. That scarcity mentality causes us to have tunnel vision, and we start seeing everything from lack.

Living in scarcity leads to a cascade of things that start happening. We start hearing those voices of "can't" or "what if" in our minds. Our cultural negativity bias flares up and then our bodies release cortisol and adrenaline, so we can fight or flee. At this point, we are not thinking. We are just reacting. We actually spend a large part of our day in this mode. That's why we are worn out and tired all the time. We were not created to live in a perpetual state of fight or flight, where our lives are in danger. Unknowingly, we have made so many things a threat to our lives. When we are living in lack, we are holding ourselves back from becoming our true selves living a life with love and joy.

To start identifying the beliefs that are really holding you back, take a look at what you believe about employment, employee/employer, supervisor, marriage, family, wife/mother, husband/father, sex, children, daughter/son, education, intelligence, and wisdom. These are some areas of our lives that seem to cause us the most conflict. I'll give you a few questions to help you on your way.

Taking Inventory of Limiting Beliefs

Let's take a look at employment. Do you believe that you should work for yourself, or do you feel like you could never own your own business? Do you believe that wage earning is bad, and you should be an entrepreneur? Do you believe that you should work for the same company for thirty years and then retire? Do you believe that you should change jobs every so often to grow, or does growth come from moving up in the same company? Is it best to have a white-collar or blue-collar job? Do you believe that you must carry on the family business? Do you believe women shouldn't work outside the home? Do you believe that being fired makes you a bad person? What does it mean to be a good employee? Do you stay at a job you don't like just for the money? Do you believe that you'll never get a good job because you don't have a good education? These are just a few questions, but they will get you started in identifying your beliefs.

The next step is to think deeper about those answers. Start asking why, and what does it mean if I don't do those things? For me I had to ask, why do I believe that being a good employee means showing up on time, never asking for a raise, doing extra work that my supervisor or co-workers ask of me, working straight through the without taking a break, and retiring from a company after working there for thirty years?

Here is my thought process as I seek my answers: I believe that showing up late is disrespectful and a good way to lose your job. For me it also means you're lazy, you're not a nice person, and you will not have any friends at work. If you lose your job, it will be difficult to get another because now you are a job hopper, and job hopping is bad. Even if you are lucky enough to find another job you won't be paid as much. I believe that being late must be punished. You must be punished because you are a bad person. Bad people get punished so they won't do those things again and they will change and be good.

Just that one belief on being late directs much of my life without my even knowing it. It causes a great conflict within me and drives me to always be on time. Let me say that being on time is "good," but it shouldn't be tied to my worth, about how I really feel about myself. Being late does not make me a bad person, but in my world, it can lead to total destruction.

As I started searching and feeling into why I had these beliefs, it took me some time and a lot of questions to really get to the bottom of things. I started with it's just the right thing to do, it's good. Culturally we have decided that being on time is good, but why does it seem like there is more for me? Why does it bring tension into my body? I have friends who are late, and they are fine with it; they don't feel the same way as I do. I actually went to my mother and asked her about being on time and she had the same answers as I did, so I seemed to get nowhere. So, I know it's tied to my worth. Somehow, if I'm getting this feeling in my body and my mind is telling me it's bad, I'm bad. I kept searching and listening for answers. Here is where the patience comes in... You never know when the answer is going to show up, but you'll know it when you hear it.

It was in a random family conversation that I learned a fact about my grandfather that I never knew. He had severe arthritis at a young age, so debilitating that he took several trips away from home for treatment. He spent my mother's eighth-grade year away from home. While my grandmother worked on and off around having children, she hadn't been the sole provider. That time while my grandfather was away was very chaotic for the family. The breadwinner was now gone, and my grandmother was feeling the pressure of providing for the family.

Hmmm, something told me, pull on this thread, Lesa... Is this where being late stems from? Women in the early 1960s were still mostly at home and limited in what was considered a woman's job. A good woman was still in the home taking care of her children. My grandmother had no choice but to become the sole breadwinner. This urgency for providing solely for the family was surrounded by fear. How long would my grandfather be gone? How would she manage? Where would she find employment? Would they hire a woman? For me, this is starting to make sense...My belief surrounding work, anything that could potentially get me fired, like being late, or not doing what my supervisor asked me, would lead to destruction of the family.

My grandmother couldn't lose her job. Her work meant the family's survival, so she would do anything to keep it. This has become the definition of a good employee for me, to sacrifice myself at all costs; but wait, why do I need to do this? I'm not a woman with a debilitated husband and two children. I'm not a woman trying to enter the workforce in the 1960s, nor have I unexpectedly become the sole breadwinner in the family. So, what is causing me to act like it's true, or soon will be? It has become the normal for my family. It's become "just what you do." The trauma, that fear and uncertainty around the situation, has become generational energy that has been passed down.

I feel the trauma of that situation to this day. While I can leave a "good" job, I have family members that are very vocal about my choices. Their fears and anxiety set into me, and I start doubting myself. I hear those voices saying you'll never get a good job again, you don't deserve it. You're no good and lazy... None of these things are true, but fear, doubt, and uncertainty are contagious. They enter our bodies and minds so easily. I can feel in my body and hear in my mind my grandmother's fear of the destruction of the family if she lost her job.

Opening Up Your Worldview

Identifying the beliefs and values that keep us limited and hold us back is an ongoing process. We have been fooled into thinking the world works in one way, our way. We tend to think that people know what we know and do what we do for the same reasons. The problem is that there is enough truth in it that we believe it because we don't question things. Most of us just take things as is because it's what we are taught. We are taught not to question, especially authority. After all, who are we?

When we aren't allowed to question or don't question our lives, it leaves us with a very narrow worldview. We should strive to keep that child's fearless curiosity, step outside of the social norms and values, to look at things from a different view. I have an inversion table that I use every day. It sits in front of a big window that looks out onto my back yard. I was so surprised what I saw in my back yard that I had never seen before and how differently things looked from that angle. When I'm inverted, I can see all the way to the top of the tree, I love looking up into the tree and seeing the birds sitting on the branches. I can't see the birds when I'm standing because the house blocks the top of the tree, but upside down I see them.

Remember what Socrates said: "The unexamined life is not worth living." Think of Carl Jung, who said, "Who looks outside, dreams; who looks inside, awakes." As we gain more understanding of ourselves and the world we live in, we can make different choices for ourselves that will bring us closer to who we really are, as opposed to who we are limited to. As we are seen, heard, and accepted for who we truly are, love builds within us and overflows from us, creating harmony in the world.

See it, Hear it, Live it

Let's connect by grounding.

1. **Stand with Your Feet on the Ground**

   Walk outside and stand barefoot on the earth, it doesn't matter whether its grass, dirt, or sand, just go with what feels right or what you have access to.

2. **Take Ten Mindful Breaths and Label Your Thoughts**

   Stand with your feet shoulder-width apart. Once you feel settled, close your eyes and slowly take in ten deep breaths. In through the nose and out through the mouth. Focus your mind on that spot below your nose and above your lips as you take in the ten deep breaths. When your mind starts to wander tell yourself, "This is just a thought," and detach from it.

3. **Focus on the Sensation of Your Feet on the Earth and Mindfully Walk**

   For a few moments, feel the sensation of your feet on the earth. Feel the connection to the earth. Once you feel connected to the earth, start slowly walking for ten paces in one direction, while gazing down with your eyes open. Move purposely. You should feel a mind-body connection as you walk. Once you have walked ten paces in one direction, turn and walk ten paces in the opposite direction.

4. **Stand Still and Take Ten Mindful Breaths**

Then stand still again, feet shoulder-width apart, and feel the earth under your feet supporting you. Now close your eyes and slowly take in ten deep breaths. In through the nose and out through the mouth. Slowly open your eyes after completing the ten breaths, then notice how your body feels for a moment before moving on.

Grounding helps bring us back to the present moment. Once you've completed this grounding meditation, you should feel calm, stable, and relaxed, but also focused.

CHAPTER 4

DRAMA TRAUMA

As I exit the limousine, I feel lifeless. A numbness comes over me as a cold chill hits my face this late March morning. I smell the scent of rain as dark clouds form in the sky. I have walked across this tarmac many times, to have lunch with the pilots, the search-and-rescue team members, and my husband. There was always laughter in the air and smiles on everyone's faces. Today will be the last time. Today is my husband's funeral. I never saw this day coming. I thought I would see my husband's contagious smile and hear the laughter in the office forever. Everything looks different today. All the officers wear dress uniforms with black sashes over their badges, and I wear a black dress. There is no laughter today—just a sense of gloom.

My heart is heavy and I long for this day to be over quickly, as we all say goodbye to my handsome, smiling Russ. As I am making my way across the tarmac, in my newly purchased black funeral dress, I look up to see a familiar face from afar. It is my husband's trainee. Time stops for a moment as our eyes meet.

At the sight of me, the widow, he is triggered into a sudden and profound sense of sorrow and disbelief. It is the same stifling feeling I have been carrying since days ago when I was notified of Russ's death. The trainee quickens his pace toward me, tears running down his face. We embrace, holding each other tightly. I feel his body trembling and his soft voice repeating, "I'm sorry, I'm so sorry, I can't believe this." I feel the depth of his heartache. I feel lost, too.

As I feel his sobs against my body, I notice that I am now comforting him. I whisper in his ear, "Everything is going to be all right. We will make it through this pain." In this moment, as I stood holding him, rocking him, and reassuring him that everything was going to be okay, I felt safe in his arms. I felt connected to Russ because of this man's love and respect for my husband. I didn't want this moment to end.

I felt a hand on my shoulder, the sheriff. "Lesa, it's time for the ceremony to start. I'll escort you to your seat." I say goodbye to the trainee and take the arm of the sheriff. We make our way through the sea of people who have come to say goodbye to Russ and we find our seats. As the procession starts, bagpipes begin to play, and tears run down my cheeks. My life has changed forever.

I didn't notice it at the time. I just did what I would always do. It wasn't until months later that I would recognize a pattern within me. Even at the worst time in my life, at a time when one would expect that I would be getting support from others, I was the one giving. This role is one of three roles in the Karpman Drama Triangle or Drama Triangle.

The Drama Triangle Roles: Rescuer, Persecutor and Victim

The Drama Triangle is a set of three roles that people take on, and move among, during emotional or high-conflict situations. These three roles, according to Dr. Stephen Karpman, are the Rescuer, the Persecutor, and the Victim. While we all have one that we favor, we do move between them all given different situations.

In my story from my husband's funeral, you can see that I was the Rescuer. In a moment when I should have been the one being comforted, I was the one giving comfort. I was comforting the trainee, treating him as the victim of the situation. This has been a lifelong pattern for me and is my go-to. I never realized how much value I got from rescuing everyone. I detest being seen as weak, so I don't show up much as a Victim, and Persecutor isn't really my style, I much prefer doing everything for everyone. The Rescuer says, "You need my help. You're not okay, but I am nice, and I will fix you."

It was only when I started to resent others that I took a step back to see why. The people I was resenting were close friends, whom I loved dearly. I would do anything for them, but I noticed that I found myself avoiding them. I had to look at myself to see why. When I looked around, I found that I had filled my life with Victims needing to be rescued, and I just couldn't keep up any longer with their demands.

Portrait of a Rescuer

You are a Rescuer when you find yourself:

- Being overly helpful
- Being overly protective
- Feeling responsible for others
- Fixing other people's problems
- Making sacrifices for others and discounting personal needs
- Keeping the victim dependent
- Rescuing to create a sense of being capable
- Always being the first to defend others

Portrait of a Victim

Let's take a look at the Victim. The Victim says, "Poor me, I give up. I'm not okay and everyone else is." You are a Victim when you find yourself:

- Feeling consistently oppressed
- Feeling helpless, ashamed
- Feeling powerless, incapable
- Dependent on others
- Seeking a rescuer
- Unable to solve problems or make decisions to help yourself
- Having a poor-me attitude
- In self-pity frequently
- Avoiding responsibility
- Viewing yourself as lesser than others

Portrait of a Persecutor

The third side of the Triangle is the Persecutor. The Persecutor says, "It's your fault. You're not okay but I am, so do what I tell you." You are a Persecutor when you find yourself being:

- Critical and judgmental
- Argumentative
- Lashing out
- Blaming others, "it's all your fault"
- Making victims feel helpless
- Driven by anger or resentment
- Using guilt to control
- Rigid in your thinking
- Bossy
- Dominating or oppressive
- Consistently having a "me first" attitude
- Always needing to be right

The child part of us, that is guided by emotion, learned as a child that the way to get their needs met or to have a sense of control in their lives is to use their behaviors to manipulate others. We first learned these roles from our families and now we play them out in all of our relationships on a subconscious level. If we are not aware of this dynamic, we will spend all our lives in the Drama Triangle, struggling and getting nowhere.

We will constantly return to those roles we played because when we are in the Drama Triangle, we have no ability to think logically. The illogical child part takes over, and we react and aren't able to think things through.

This leaves us only to stay chained in those patterns of unhealthy behaviors and weak boundaries.

All-or-nothing thinking and language is a good indicator that a person is in the Drama Triangle, language like, "You always..." "You never..." "Your entire day..." The following hypothetical story shows the Drama Triangle in action.

Ted's Drama Story

Ted's job has been extremely busy lately. Ted is called into his boss' office to discuss some recent mistakes that he has made. The boss yells at Ted and tells him if he makes one more mistake this quarter he will be fired. Ted is distraught so he tries calling his wife, but she doesn't answer. He realizes that it is Tuesday, her day for running errands. He gets upset and says, "I've told her a thousand times to take her cell phone with her, but she never remembers!"

Ted arrives home to a messy house, his wife on the phone washing dishes, one child at the kitchen table doing homework, one child practicing the violin upstairs, and the youngest child chasing the dog around the house. When his wife gets off the phone, this is the conversation that takes place:

> Ted: Where have you been all day?!
>
> Wife: It's Tuesday. You know I run errands. I've been busy, Ted! You don't have to yell!
>
> Ted: I almost got fired today and I couldn't even get ahold of you! (yelling at the kids) Can't you kids shut up for one minute? why is this place always so messy?! (kids start to cry)

Wife: Kids, it's okay. It's not your fault. Dad just had a bad day at work. (yelling at Ted) I am always protecting the kids from you and your bad temper, and I'm sick of it! You are angry all the time!

Ted: Well thanks a lot! I get yelled at by my boss and now you, just great!

Wife: At least you are with adults during the day. All I ever have to talk to are the kids!

Kids: We promise we will be good. Stop fighting! Stop fighting!

Wife: Now Ted look what you have done!

Ted: I'm the bad guy?! I work hard all day, and no one cares or even appreciates me! It's always about the tough life you and the kids have. I'm the one who provides for you all. You think I could get a little respect like the other husbands—but not in this house, oh no! This is the house from hell. See you later!

This dramatic exit makes the perfect setting for the wife and kids to rescue Ted later that night. This story is just one way in which the Drama Triangle can look, intense with a lot of yelling, but it can also have a passive/aggressive dynamic as well.

Triple Trouble

I'm sure this sounds familiar, as we spend so much of our lives in this dynamic without even knowing it. We subconsciously attract someone to fill the role we need, because living in the Drama Triangle makes us feel less vulnerable and gives us a sense of control. When we are in the Drama Triangle, we can avoid the truth about ourselves and others. We can keep those deep-seated fears and emotions buried for years.

It takes a lot on our part to move out of the Triangle, as the other person doesn't want to lose their counterpart either. They will do everything in their power to keep us in this dynamic. Conflict is the quickest, easiest way to keep us engaged. It can be difficult to be vulnerable and feel like we are going to be rejected, alone, or abandoned by those we love.

As we move from the child part of ourselves and into our adult frame of mind, that logical part that is able to reason, acknowledge our emotions, and work through our fears, we gain a sense of empowerment and freedom in our lives. We are able to more quickly identify those old patterns, develop new ones, and create healthy boundaries for ourselves. Here are the steps you can take.

5. **Recognize the drama.**

Become aware of your behaviors. This is definitely a process; some of it is easy and some of it is difficult. First, we must become aware of our thought processes and understand them. Do you hear yourself using that all-or-nothing language? "I always..." "You never..." You are most likely in the Drama Triangle.

6. **Become aware of your body.**

The Drama Triangle definitely plays out in our bodies. Listen to your body; it speaks to you every day. What are you physically complaining about? Does your back or knee hurt? Do you get an upset stomach? Do you get frequent headaches or migraines? Take a look at what is going on at the time you notice them. I have a friend who will start feeling helpless and get this deep sick feeling in the pit of her stomach when she is going into the victim role. When I go into my rescuer role, my lower back will start hurting. It's as if I'm carrying the weight of the world on me. When I play the victim, I can barely breathe. I feel like a weight is on my chest. I struggle to take a deep breath. I have to consciously stop and take a moment, telling myself I am not a victim. I have options, I am the creator of my life. I have also noticed when someone is trying to get me to play into the triangle, I get this sharp, stabbing pain under my right shoulder blade and it takes my breath away.

7. **Seek alternatives.**

Start to list your options. This has become one way thinking for most of us and we don't even know or see that there could be other ways to react to situations. It does help to stop and think of your situation as you would for a friend. What advice would you give them? It helps take you out of the situation. This will take a little time to do. In the beginning you might not be able to keep yourself out of the Drama Triangle, but it will get easier.

You are most likely not even going to know that you were in the Drama Triangle until after the situation is over and done, but you can go back through it after the fact. You will be able to remember what you were thinking at the time and then develop other options you could have taken. Be kind to yourself as you work through this process. I would get so frustrated at myself when I knew I was going in and couldn't stop myself from doing it. There's nothing worse than seeing the wreck happen in real time. I had to start looking at it as I got closer to overcoming it instead of being overtaken by it.

8. Find your alignment.

Ask: Does this feel right for me? To do this, you will need to look at what you value and what is important to you. What brings you peace? What makes you happy? Take your time with this. Don't get caught up with what the Rescuer, Victim, or Persecutor feels is value. You might need to look up a list of values to even get started and that's okay. Remember, you have the right to change your list at any time. That is what growing does—it changes you.

As we grow, we are going to be making changes in our lives. All the changes we make may have some negative outcomes, so we will need to be aware of the risks involved, make our conscious choice, and then accept the outcome. Accepting the risks is the fourth step. Remember you are not that child any longer who only had limited choices. You are an adult with a lot more capabilities and a lot more options.

9. Make your choice.

Your choice should not only reflect your values, what is important to you, but it must also keep you out of the Drama Triangle. This will all take time and a little effort on your part, but it is totally worth it. You will be surprised how much better you will feel out of the drama triangle and how much more fulfilling your relationships will become.

Your life will be so much more rewarding and satisfying when you get outside of the Drama Triangle, shaping the Victim into the Creator, the Persecutor into the Challenger, and the Rescuer into the Coach. Let's take a look at what the Creator, the Challenger, and the Coach look like.

- Victim → Creator
- Persecutor → Challenger
- Rescuer → Coach

From Victim to Creator

We become the Creator with problem solving. Identifying what you want in your life, seeing your options, and then taking action to achieve what you want, will bring power back into your life. Your first step is to recognize and acknowledge the potential of being the creator in your life, then identifying what you have control over and what you don't. We really only have control over our own thoughts, feeling, and actions—everything else is up for grabs. Creators focus on what they want in life, as opposed to victims who focus on what they don't want. Creators understand the flow of life, and that everything is constantly changing, so they don't attach themselves to a certain, or right, way. Because they are outcome-driven, they can hold the dynamic tension of the unknown and focus on what they want and how they choose to respond to life events.

Creators are continuously refining their truths by focusing on questions like these: What do I most care about? What are my values? What is the outcome I want, given the current reality? To move out of the victim mindset, we must learn to take full responsibility for our response to life's events. You must really know your values and what you want in your life. If you don't, it will be easy to fall back into blaming others or feeling powerless.

As you start searching yourself for these values and desires in life, it's important to understand that fear will creep in. You are starting to be seen, heard, and loved, which can leave you feeling unsafe. When that happens, talk to yourself as you would to a good friend, and ask yourself: And if that were possible? What do I want right now in life? How can I feel safe as I explore my dreams? To create my dreams, where must I take responsibility?

I know that in the beginning you might not even know what you want your life to look like or what you like to do. You most likely have not really connected with yourself for a long time. I had this dilemma. I had to go back to my childhood to start. What did I like to play? What did I spend my time doing? You can really start anywhere—just start. We are very good at waiting for the right time, or when we will have more time. This I know for sure: do it now! There will never be a right or perfect time in our minds—we can always find an excuse.

Remember, all these choices are not set in stone. You can change your mind at any point and go in the total opposite direction if that is what you want. It's your journey. You do not have to travel the path that everyone is on.

You really already know your path—it's in you, it just needs to be uncovered. To do this, tell yourself, "Let me try this, then evaluate it, adjust if necessary, step back, then take another step forward."

From Persecutor to Challenger

We become the Challenger through clear structure. Challengers see others as Creators. They know their values and what is important to them. They set firm boundaries, listen actively to others, and ask questions, unlike their counterparts who blame and judge. Challengers see the world as a place to learn and grow. They know their worth, but value others' ideas.

Challengers are courageous. They are not afraid to step outside the box. They are great at seeing things from a different perspective. They focus on the underlying limiting beliefs that others may be unconscious to but are acting out of. They ask, "What are the assumptions being held?" Challengers see the bigger picture and not the details. They are attuned to their intuition and are guided by it.

The key to move from the role of Persecutor to Challenger is to let go of your ego—the need to be right. Someone once asked me, do you want to be right, or do you want to be happy? I have never forgotten that. In the role of Persecutor, we fear becoming a Victim if we are not in control. We will control, protect, and defend ourselves at all costs in order to avoid that. As a result, Persecutors believe that their way is right and the best way, but they tend to overestimate their abilities and expertise.

To move into the role of Challenger, you must become comfortable with creative chaos and your own insecurity. You must believe the world is a safe place to step into the role of Challenger. You can only do this one step at a time. As a Challenger you will need to develop and nurture compassion for those who are different from you. You will need to put yourself in new situations to become comfortable in them. By putting yourself in new situations you will use parts of yourself that call for your creativity and diversity as you respond, while learning to be calm in the face of uncertainty.

From Rescuer to Coach

We become Coach using clear support. Coaches see others as co-creators, knowing others are capable of caring for themselves. Coaches are curious, compassionate, and supportive. They trust the process of discovery and hold the space as others tap into the wisdom that lies within themselves.

A Coach endeavors to catch their own judgmental thoughts and to suspend them. Coaches ask, "What am I not seeing here?" They allow the process to unfold instead of pushing to make it happen. They trust the process and ask powerful and direct questions for clarity of outcome.

To move into the role of Coach, a Rescuer must let go of their deep need for external acceptance and love. Rescuers believe that others value them for their good deeds of saving or fixing things. Rescuing has become the way to receive the acceptance and love they covet.

Moving from Rescuer to Coach, you will need to cultivate self-acceptance and become aware of the internal rescuing behaviors. Because you have spent a life dedicated to taking care of others, it is essential that you start taking care of yourself. Compassionate self-care is necessary for you to move out of the Rescuer and into the coach role. Developing radical forgiveness, self-love, and body awareness will allow you to feel worthy, whole and complete. Then you will be able to see the gifts that others genuinely possess.

Being gentle with ourselves can help mitigate those Drama Triangles we create within ourselves. You know the ones where you start beating yourself up for something that didn't go just right in your day. Say hello to your Persecutor. Just as that voice gets going, your Victim says, "They always treat me badly," and you start to feel sorry for yourself. Now your Rescuer steps in and says it's okay, "Let's just have some cookies. You'll feel better then."

When we a take a moment before we react in any situation, it gives us the time to check in with ourselves and break out of those patterns that we are unknowingly following. If we look into the dark places within ourselves, we can make another choice when we see patterns that no longer serve us. It's in the darkness that we can find our brightest light to shine in the world.

Understanding ourselves and the world we live in takes time. Self-compassion goes a long way here. Be kind and loving to yourself as you navigate these new challenges. Give yourself permission to laugh instead of listening to that critic that will certainly show up. Most of all, trust the process.

See it, Hear it, Live it

Let's connect by writing a love letter to ourselves.

Self-care is something most of us don't do often enough. How often do you think about loving yourself? We are often extremely hard on ourselves, so take a moment to tell yourself all the great things you are doing. Our thoughts become our reality.

Take ten minutes and write a love letter to yourself. Be sure to include your whole self, your body, mind, and spirit. Before you start writing, close your eyes, put your hand over your heart, and take a few deep breaths. When you feel ready open your eyes and write whatever comes to mind. Don't overthink it.

Here are a few prompts to get you started:

What I wish for you is...

You make my day when you...

I love you because...

What makes you different from anyone else is...
You are beautiful because...
Let's make a date to...

However you choose to start, make sure to love on every aspect of yourself.

CHAPTER 5

THE GAME OF LIFE

It's nearing the end of my senior year of high school, and everyone is asking me what I'm going to do next. The truth is I have no idea. I haven't really had much time to think about anything. My parents divorced about a year ago and the family is still adjusting. My siblings and I all stayed with my mom and really haven't seen much of my dad since the divorce. He keeps promising to come see us, but it never seems to work out.

Being the oldest child, I am taking on more responsibility for my three sisters because my mom is now working. We move to a place that is affordable. We move from our house in the country, where we all had our own rooms, to a low-income area of Kankakee, Illinois, where we share a house with another family. They live downstairs and we live upstairs. My two youngest sisters share a room with bunk beds. Mom shares a room with my other sister, and I get the sunporch because it is the smallest room.

I hate living in town. I miss my connection with nature—living in town is all about concrete and asphalt. I feel so disconnected. The move into town means that I have a longer commute to school, but that is okay. I'm just happy that I don't have to change schools my senior year and graduate with a bunch of kids I don't even know.

In addition to the move, and caring for my three sisters, a new brother is on the way. I am like a mother to my siblings, taking on the role in the family. I am doing what any mother would. I make sure everyone has clean clothes to wear to school, so I wash clothes, fold, and put them away. I keep the house as clean as you can with five kids, which means daily vacuuming and mopping the floors at least once a week. I am constantly picking up after everyone. I make the dinners, so I put the kids in the car and go grocery shopping. I get a lot of looks from people shopping because they assume the kids are mine. It makes me so mad when people make snide comments. I do what needs to be done to get by.

I fake a lot of what I think I am supposed to do next. I look on at what others are doing, and it seems like most of the girls are looking to get married. I don't even have a boyfriend, so marriage seems out of the question for me. Some of the more popular girls with money are going to college after school so that's what I say I am going to do. After all, no one would know if I did or not.

I graduate with honors from high school. It doesn't matter that I am a good student—I know we don't have the money for me to go to college. I talk to my mother about it anyway, and we work out a way for me to get a Pell Grant so I can go to the community college.

In all these questions from everyone at this time of my life, there seemed to be a set design to what was to come next in my life. It made me feel like there was something wrong with me because I didn't know what was next.

I have never really had a chance to find out. I never had the chance to dream about what I wanted in life. My reality was to make sure my siblings and I survived, which is a common reality for many. We take on the fears and struggles of our parents and don't really get to dream. Even if you don't have the struggles I did, there is a certain way to do things. A set of "nexts" for you to do.

I have always felt like I was never enough. I never seemed to have the right background, the right parents, the right education, or the right employment. I was never pretty enough, outgoing enough, or talented enough. At best, I was average and felt unseen for most of my life.

Suddenly all these things seemed to start to matter more, like what clothes you wore, how pretty you were, how smart you were, where your parents were employed or how much money they made—my world was falling apart. The fall I turned thirteen, my grandmother died, forcing us to move away from my childhood home on the river. We moved to a small rural township with about fifty people. The place was known as "where the bad people lived." I was devastated. I think I grieved the whole time we lived there. It wasn't an easy time for anyone, as my parents' marriage disintegrated. I was sixteen when the divorce finally happened. It was the time when I should have been going to prom and homecoming, but that didn't happen for me.

My mom and I switched roles in the family. She became the one with the new boyfriends, as she tried to make sense of what happened in the divorce. She would wear my clothes and go out on dates while I stayed home with the kids. We fought. One night after dinner, my sister and I were doing the dishes and my mom came through to tell us she was going out. I lost it and threw a plate at her.

It hit the door and broke all over the floor—now I had a mess to clean up. I was furious.

Unknowingly, I was feeling the pull of what I like to call the "pillars of life"—religion, family, marriage, education, and employment. These are a few of the bigger constructs from which we draw our worth. They impact all of us to a degree. Let's take a look at a few.

Love, Marriage, and a Baby carriage

Marriage and family, they go hand in hand. Whether we want to admit it or not, we all believe that we should get married and have children—it's just what you do. The social constructs tell us that if we are good enough, we will find that perfect spouse and have perfect children.

This sets us up for failure. Relationships in any form take effort, and they certainly are not perfect. It leaves those who are single wondering why. *What did I do wrong not to get someone who loves me and wants to be with me?* It also leaves those who are married but struggling wondering the same thing. *What did I do wrong? Why isn't this marriage going like it should?*

It—the perfect marriage—has become so ingrained in us that we don't even give it a second thought. If we were given the choice, I believe that there are many people who would choose not to marry or have children, but when it is tied to our value, we simply have no choice. Each of these unseen forces have a hold on us, as they all reinforce that we are never enough. Each of these are a block in the "one-wall prison" that we create for ourselves based on our beliefs.

All these pillars have the "best" and "only way" attached to them. If you're good enough, then this is how your life is supposed to look. We struggle all our lives to be right and good enough. These have become the unseen forces of the "it's just what you do" mentality.

It's like how trainers use rope to tie the leg of small elephants to hold them still. As they grow, they are conditioned to believe that they cannot break free. The now-grown elephants are mighty but believe that the rope can hold still hold them, so they never try to break away. Like the elephants, how many of us go through life holding onto a belief that we can't do something simply because we failed once, or someone told us we couldn't do it?

Religion's hold on us has deep roots tied to our eternal worth. If we aren't in the "right" religion, we may be going to hell for all eternity. Marriage and family keep us bound to the "one way" mentality. There is still a long-held belief in this world today that a family consists of a man, a woman, and their children. We had to take this pillar to the U.S. Supreme Court to be challenged. If you aren't married or don't have children, you are now not enough somehow because we have set a "best" way to define family.

Educated, and Accepted

Higher education binds us to the "only way" to get ahead. If we don't have an Ivy League education, then we aren't going anywhere in life. We all want to get into those schools because somehow they make us better than someone who goes to the local university. The elite schools are supposed to get us better jobs, better connections, and more money, leading us to believe that we are better people than those who don't. This creates a cultural divide between the haves and have nots.

The 40-hour Prison

Employment has its own special way of imprisoning us. Most of us end up in jobs that we don't like and stay because it's just easier. We aren't even sure how we ended up there, but now we stay because of money, whether or not we feel like it is enough. Most of never get the chance to find out what we really want to do in life. We are led to what the culture values and how much money we can make in that field.

I believe that if we are given the chance to find our passion, no matter what it is, we will be fulfilled, creativity will flow, and abundance will follow. If washing cars is your thing and you are given the freedom to fully engage in it, you will be in love with life. As a result, creativity will flow from your soul and something awesome will come forth, bringing the abundance that we all look for in life. When we are fully engaged with something we love, time seems to fly by. Think about what you could create doing that thing you love every day—I'm sure it would be amazing. I know when I see someone engaged in what she loves, it makes me want it.

These pillars become our guidance system, and we get our value from them. We don't understand that the whole system is set for us to fail. The Dominator style of our culture sets up a struggle between who is on top and who is on the bottom. There will always be someone with more, and it causes us to feel less-than. There is nothing wrong with competition, but when everything has become tied to our worth, it forces us into a kill-or-be-killed mentality. We can never see the whole picture at one time. It takes time and effort to put all the pieces together. We literally have to destroy the thing that we desperately want. We have to be willing to lose everything, so we can gain everything.

We have to destroy the social constructs, but we don't even really know they exist and how they impact us. We must destroy the value menu, and create a new one, because until we do, that list of values seems the only way to success and worth for us. Our limiting beliefs must be destroyed, killing off the "can't do" mentality. We must identify and end the game of life that the pillars of the social constructs have erected.

The social constructs are a powerful force in our lives that hold us captive. But just seeing the social constructs is not enough to get ourselves out of them. We can know about the pillars of the constructs—religion, marriage, family, education, and employment—but we need to understand how we act within them and what we believe about them to really release their hold.

Have you ever wondered why the same thing keeps happening in your life? Do you even see the patterns in your life? I'm sure you can see it in other people's lives. You know that friend who is dating the guy who takes advantage of her kindness, then leaves her? She always seems to find him. How about that one coworker whom everyone tries to avoid because he always needs something?

As children, we learned to use patterns of manipulation to get our needs met and have a sense of control in our lives. We learned these roles from our families and still play them out in our adult relationships on a subconscious level. Most of us have never heard of the Drama Triangle, yet it plays out in every interaction and relationship we have until we are aware of if it.

Forces at Play

To break free, we must dismantle the vicious cycles of the Drama Triangle. We must replace Victim with Creator, Persecutor with Challenger, and Rescuer with Coach. All those voices and fears we hear in our minds, that have come from our parents and authority figures telling us that we are never enough, must be quelled so we can hear our whisper of truth. We must be willing to reconnect to our disembodied selves to feel the truth within and create flow around us.

The COVID-19 pandemic changed the landscape of our lives, and we are still struggling to get our footing. It has caused disconnection and uncertainty, and it pitted us against one another. It brought to the surface all of our fears and insecurities, so that when we meet up against someone who is different, we enter the Drama Triangle to defend ourselves, with the kill-or-be-killed ideals of the Dominator culture.

The social constructs at large remain unseen. We have been led to believe that these constructs are best for us. We are taught not to question them. After all, who do you think you are to offer an opinion on something of that magnitude? These constructs seem to be set in stone; they have become "just what you do."

We all get caught up in the value menu of the social constructs. We get our worth from how many items we have from that list. It has become the one size fits all. Our fears and insecurities, taught to us by the Dominator style of our culture, take over, giving us our set of limiting beliefs. These beliefs of "can't do" play right into the pillars of the social constructs, creating our self-imposed one-wall prison. We defend ourselves in that prison with a never-ending cycle of playing the Drama Triangle. That drama causes us to blame others, not valuing their opinions; to manipulate others, feeling powerless within ourselves; or to appear self-sacrificing, feeling that others need our help, devaluing that other person's capacity to help themselves. The voices that have gotten into our subconscious seem to reinforce our limiting beliefs and tell us we will never be enough. As those voices grow in volume, our fears and insecurities set in and cause our bodies to respond with the fight-or-flight response. It's only when we get that big shock that we feel connected to our bodies again. We have been numbing our pain for so long that we have chronically disconnected from our bodies, and when we are disconnected from ourselves, there is no way we can have a meaningful connection with anyone else.

I love the lyrics of Etiquette's song "Attention Seeker" ... *Simple conversation, is a land-mine field, tread lightly...* This is what happens when all these pillars align, and we can never seem to feel good about ourselves. Have you ever been in a conversation and noticed a change in the air, and you are wondering what just happened? What did I just miss? It's likely that someone has unknowingly gotten triggered in the conversation and is now fully engaged in the Drama Triangle.

A couple of my big triggers are being seen as dumb or weak, and I use the Rescuer from the Drama Triangle to defend myself. It's so funny that I am the only one who sees me in that light. No one who knows me would ever describe me as weak or dumb. Actually, the opposite is true. They all say that I'm very intelligent and one of the emotionally strongest people they know. The dumb and weak ideas about myself came early in life and were reinforced when I started kindergarten. I believed my teacher when she told me I was so dumb that I couldn't even tie my own shoes. At that young age, teachers know everything and couldn't possibly be wrong.

The Experiment

The Stanford Prison Experiment,(SPE) which took place in August 1971, is a great example of how this game shows up in life. The SPE was a social psychology study in which college students became prisoners or guards in a simulated prison environment. It was intended to measure the effect of role-playing, labeling, and social expectations on behavior over a two-week period. The experiment was terminated on the sixth day due to the emotional breakdowns of the prisoners and the excessive aggression of the guards. This experiment reveals how people will readily conform to the social roles they are expected to play, especially if they are strongly stereotyped.

It is so easy for us to fall into our roles of the social construct as seen from the Stanford Prison Experiment. Take a moment and think of how many roles you play in your life... daughter, sister, mother, wife, firstborn, youngest child, co-worker, teacher, failure, golden child... the list goes on. All these social roles have unseen duties, obligations, and expectations that go along with each. We have become so accustomed to them in our lives that they remain hidden from us.

If you haven't seen the movie of the Stanford Prison Experiment, you might want to watch it. It is very eye opening. It helps to understand how we can find ourselves in situations that we would have never thought we could be in. The character of Jesse Fletcher, played by the actor Nelsan Ellis, is a good example of what can happen to us. His character is a former prisoner that Dr. Zimbardo, the psychologist that conducted the Standard Prison Experiment, brings in to evaluate the authenticity of the experiment. Ellis' character turns into a person hated; he became the people he despised in prison. That can happen to us when we aren't able to see all those unseen forces that are moving us about and holding us back. They all start acting upon us and we are overtaken by the chorus of their voices.

The social constructs, as an authority, set up the program for us to follow, then teaches us not to question it. After all, an authority knows what's best for us, so we just follow along with the program even when it isn't working for us, believing that we just need to be better.

As we are giving our best but falling short, we defend ourselves the only way we know how- through the Drama Triangle. Defending ourselves because of our need to be right has become a way of life for most. When we are not in the Drama Triangle, there's no need for that defense. Being right is no longer tied to our value. We can see that our opinion is just as valuable as another's even when our opinions are different.

Because we are just reacting to situations on autopilot from an old pattern learned in childhood and we're not conscious of that, we can never get out of this cycle. As adults we have outgrown these learned behaviors, but we still act out of them because we have done them for so long and don't even see them in ourselves. Because we don't question the social constructs and we are just reacting to situations, we will never feel empowered in our lives. We have already given that power over, but we don't see it.

For us to release the hold of these pillars of the social construct, we first need to see them, acknowledge their power in our lives, set out to identify how they entered our lives, work through how they show up for us, and finally realize that there is another way to live our lives.

The social construct and the Drama Triangle work hand in hand, keeping us in a never-ending cycle of misery. The social constructs set up the foundation of what is valuable, what is right or wrong, good or bad. That leads us to measure ourselves against it. We ask ourselves, what don't I have from what the social constructs say I should have? There is usually a lot and that makes us feel less-than, and therein begins the need to defend ourselves.

Because we have not been taught any different, we use what we know and go back to our childhood remedies to soothe and defend ourselves. The Victim, Rescuer, and Persecutor are the social norm, and we don't see anything wrong with them. We can't see the Persecutor when we yell at our spouse, "You are always late," or "you never pick up after yourself!" For most of us, being late, messy, or lazy is labeled as bad, so we feel like it's justifiable. Good trumps bad every time.

The thing is we don't realize that we all see things differently. One person's trash is another person's treasure. We all use the social constructs to support and reject who we have been taught to be and use the Drama Triangle to bolster that identity. In that Triangle, there are losers and winners, just as the Dominator style of the social construct has told us, so it seems right.

Most of us are going to find it difficult at first because we won't want to give up those things that give us our worth. We won't be able to see another way because we have been so fooled into believing the "one way." We won't want another way because this way seems just easier, but we must be willing to let go so new things can come into our lives.

We need to think of it as a scene from a movie, where we are sifting through the rubble of our lives. It's a scene of total destruction where nothing is familiar, and it feels very uncomfortable to be there. It's going to look like the set of a horror sci-fi movie gone bad. We must walk through the rubble, picking out pieces to see where or if they fit us. The landscape at first is dark and scary. We are going to get some bumps and bruises as we navigate this scene, but it is so worth it in the end. We will have a life that we could have never imagined, one full of light, fulfillment, and abundance. We will ask ourselves, "Why didn't I do this sooner?"

See it, Hear it, Live it

Let's connect by moving our bodies.

Let's dance... Put on your favorite music and move.

Dance is a great way to get those feelings from our emotions moving. When we are in the drama triangle and get triggered, those feelings get stuck in our bodies. As they say, the body keeps the score.

Dance gives your emotions space to exist, to move, and to change. It can provide a time and space for insights into why you might be feeling the way you do and how to better deal with it. Your emotions can become tools that bring you closer to your personal power and improve your relationships as you release those triggers through dance.

Don't worry if you're not a dancer—just move. Let your body move you. Don't think about it. Feel the freedom and space in your body. Feel the energy in your body flow and expand. Close your eyes and dance like no one is watching.

CHAPTER 6

LISTEN AND BE HEARD

t's Friday evening, my assignment is due tomorrow, and I'm struggling, to the point of meltdown. I'm taking an online class to get my certification to become an English as a Second Language teacher and teach English abroad. This is the third week of class and I have to develop a lesson plan for a beginning ESL class for adults.

I have never taught before, so lesson planning is new to me. I don't know what I'm doing or even where to look for help. I have looked at the examples in our coursework, but it just doesn't seem to make sense to me. I decide I'm just going to quit the class and admit once again that I did something stupid. *I wasted that $1,500, I'm not cut out for this. I'm just not smart enough to be a teacher.*

I write a post on the class forum expressing my feelings of inadequacy and desire to quit because I just can't seem to figure all this out. I was expecting to get the confirmation that I'm not enough and should just quit. However, to my surprise, I actually had a lot of students tell me that they were feeling the same way. They encouraged me to press on, one step at a time, and that I definitely could succeed.

As a result of their support, I didn't feel so alone, and I was able to gather myself and complete the assignment. I created my first lesson plan, one of many for the course, and turned it in on time. In the end, I did really well in the course and received my ESL certification.

Say What?

- *Who do you think you are?*
- *What did you think you were going to do?*
- *Did you really think that you were smart enough to take that class?*
- *See I told you that you couldn't do it, that you would fail.*
- *Now look at yourself, you have spent a lot of money on something stupid, just like you.*
- *How are you going to have money for milk or shoes for the kids?*
- *What a loser you are! Just quit already so you don't embarrass yourself any more than you already have.*
- *You just aren't very smart.*
- *You don't have what it takes to make it. Just end it and put yourself out of misery.*
- *You know you can't do it.*

This is what all the voices in my head were telling me as I started into my third week of class. Where do all these voices in our heads come from? Do we even recognize they are there? Most of us don't even give them a second thought because we have had them for so long.

Not only did I start listening to those voices in my head, but I believed them fully. I never questioned their being wrong. That led me to fall right into Victim from the Drama Triangle. The Victim was telling me, *Poor Lesa, she isn't very smart, just like her teacher told her. She will never be enough. She can't do things right the first time, so she is no good.*

We seem to have such a self-critical mind. We are constantly telling ourselves what we did wrong. Sometimes it is so hard to find our own voice amongst all those tapes that are playing. We have had most of those voices for a long time and they seem to have melded into one chorus that is familiar.

Those voices start when we are young. Have you ever heard of a mantra? For most of us when we hear the word, we think of some weird Eastern thing that monks do or maybe some yoga-type people. Some word we can't understand that is repeated over and over again. A mantra is a word or phrase that is repeated to help the body and mind find peace. I believe that our Western world has its mantras, but for the most part, they go unseen.

Think about some of the things you were told as a child or that you tell your children. I think one of the first ones we are told is shhhh. We even get a visual cue as our parent puts their index finger in front of their mouth for more reinforcement. Have you heard the early bird gets the worm or money doesn't grow on trees? How about these:

Big boys don't cry.

Little girls should be seen and not heard.

As children, we don't fully come into our analytical minds until about age twelve. Because a child's mind doesn't have the capacity to edit all the things that come into it, children are very programmable and easily influenced. All these beliefs and values flood the mind and are taken on as our very own, without us knowing they come from an eternal source.

You can start to see where all the voices in your mind come from. We don't stop to think where all the things that are in our minds come from. We never realize that they are not our own Most of us just take them as normal. Everyone has them, and that is true, but they don't have to control us. These thoughts are destroying us, and we don't even know it. They cause us to think and do things that if we were aware of them, most of us wouldn't do.

Most of us have these voices floating around in our heads and it has become normal to hear them. We listen to them as if they are our own thoughts, and we act on them without even knowing. All these programs that have been instilled in us run in the background. They seem so normal because they have been designed by that bigger power of the social constructs and passed down. We end up taking all those voices we hear as truths.

We all have these programs instilled in us, but they can look a little bit different and cause us to do different things; that's why they are so difficult to see. I was told by an authority figure that I wasn't very smart, and to this very day I am affected by that comment. Someone else might have just blown it off, but I, and my journey up to that point in time, had already been layered with *you aren't very smart*. I don't believe that adults know the power of their words, especially to children during those critical formative years. I doubt many people know about brain wave pattern development. It is just not something that is mainstream or taught to us as children.

Our social constructs have set up a system, those beliefs, labels, and actions that make us worthy, that tell us how valuable we are. The more we have in our lives off that menu the better we feel about ourselves, as we have been taught to get our worth from an external source.

We all seek those things, but it seems as though we are all still missing something. I think it's because we know that those things don't make us worthy, but we don't have anything else to build on because we have been fooled into believing it. Mark Twain once said, «It's easier to fool people than convince them that they have been fooled."

A friend has been in and out of a relationship with a guy now for over a year. She knows that she really doesn't want the relationship, yet she can't let it go. She says it's better than nothing and she feels safe to have him in her "back pocket." I realized that a lot of women do this because we have been fooled into thinking that a man keeps us safe, both physically and emotionally.

I stayed for many years in my second marriage for a lot of those same reasons. It's better than nothing, until it's not. As the pain got more intense and as I listened more to my inner self, I found the courage to leave my second husband. We divorced, I gave him everything and moved out. Ironically, he never saw it coming. It was about a year before we spoke again. We both grew a lot in that year. Space was good for both of us, and we are now friends again. But I had to find the courage to leave, to be alone.

We have been told for years that women are the weaker sex and not to go out alone. This is where that has taken us. The social construct surrounding the roles of men and women has been lying to us for years.

We even do these things to ourselves. Those voices in our minds are lying to us. What do your voices tell you that isn't true? *I'll never get married, I'll never lose the weight, I always say the wrong thing...*When we hear ourselves using the words always or never, that's a cue for us to stop and challenge that message—it's most likely a voice that is limiting us in some way. We have such a self-critical and negative mindset running our lives.

Take a moment and think about the last time you were kind to yourself or had a nice thought about yourself. We may have done ten good things in a day, but we will rarely see them. Even if we do, we will focus on that one thing that we feel we could have done better. This is called the negativity bias. It is our propensity not only to see negative experiences but to focus on them more readily. This bias is due to our past need to survive. When it was a matter of life and death, we were on high alert all the time. Our brains still work in that way even though those threats are not real for us any longer.

It's all about really understanding yourself and the social constructs that are moving the world. We don't even think about where these constructions come from. We just follow along. Even if we think we are bucking the system, we have just swung to the other side of the spectrum, which is really the opposite side of the same coin, so to speak. Nothing has really changed. We really need to seek balance, but no one has ever told us about that, and we have no idea what it looks like or feels like.

We have become accustomed to the feeling that those voices give us. It feels comfortable. We actually seek it— this is called homeostasis. As crazy as it sounds, if we were hit every day growing up, that would be normal to us. We think everyone gets hit. Sometimes that hit even turns into a form of love that we will seek out. That's how much that imprinting as a child means to us later in life. Even if we don't seek out someone who hits us, most of the time we are withdrawn and withhold from others, so there is no real connection either.

Those voices have told us all in so many ways and for so long that we are never good enough. We just need one more thing, one more degree, one more investment, or whatever it might be for us to be good enough, but when we get there, it still doesn't give us the feeling we are desiring. It always seems like somewhere else is always better and more is all we'll ever need. So, we keep pursuing something that doesn't exist. Those voices are very powerful, and our bodies actually get involved so it feels real.

What we are actually looking for is a feeling, and we search in very specific ways for it. I have lost about eighty pounds in this past year. About the time I was getting to my goal weight, I started gaining weight back. I was so upset. The voices told me, *It's okay. It's just a little weight and you have been so good. You deserve it. Besides, it's the holidays. Relax a little.* There is truth to all that, but I had not realized that I had just given the keys of the bus over to a voice that was terrified and going to drive us over a cliff.

I have two voices that are very powerful. One tells me I'm dumb, and the other tells me I'm weak. Neither of them is true, but I have lived my whole life as if they were. I have been stepping out of my comfort zone, so a lot of the time my voices are screaming, but I have been able to manage them. I have been challenging those voices so much that I have been keeping them all off balance and that is very uncomfortable for them. They wanted to return to the power seat, so they ramped up their volume and connections within me.

My voices of the all-or-nothing perfectionist uncovered my belief that I will always be overweight, and that got me. That chorus of voices told me that I lack self-control. If only I could control myself, I wouldn't be overweight, so I subconsciously ate more. Which led me to believe that

I have no self-control, so I beat myself up, believing that I was weak. I never for a moment during the time the voices were speaking to me realized that I had lost the weight. I do have what it takes to succeed.

In believing those voices, I was paralyzed, and I unconsciously stopped the flow of energy in my body and held on to it. I kept asking myself, *What is different? Why am I struggling now with my eating habits?* The answer took me weeks to sort out. It happened when I made the connection between the voices of the all-or-nothing perfectionist and the one that told me I was weak. In exposing those voices, I was able to change my thought patterns around them.

I realized that I also have a belief that being seen and heard leads directly to trouble. When I am overweight, I feel like I'm hidden. I go unseen under all that weight, and under all those big clothes. That's why when I get close to my goal or success, I sabotage myself. I subconsciously don't know who I would be without being overweight. Being seen is terrifying.

My belief that perfection is the only way to be good enough is paralyzing because I know I'm not perfect. So, if being perfect is the only way to be good enough, I know I'm a fraud and will never measure up. That leaves me with only one answer: I will never be good enough and will always be unworthy.

The closer I get to being seen and heard, the fiercer those voices become. They will do anything to maintain their power over me. Personal growth is a process of understanding and re-understanding. It's like peeling back the layers of an onion with another layer being exposed. The struggle is worth the end result. Remember, it only takes one degree of change to end up in a different direction.

The Rebirth

During growth, our voices shift and take different forms, and they all die in some fashion. I like to think of myself as a mandala—all the roles, labels, and more—that makes me who I am. I used to destroy those parts of me that I didn't want to see or hear any longer, but I realized that they are a part of me and in rejecting them I really wasn't honoring myself. So, I started this practice of loving compassion for them. They all get the opportunity to join the expanded Lesa and move forward to a new exciting way of being.

I have developed a ritual that I do when I ask them to step aside and make way for the new. First, I feel where in my body that belief or voice is held. I usually get an age of when the belief, trauma, or voice was born and was stored in my body, so I ask that Lesa to remove it from my body. I ask her to remove it and place it in my hands. Then I thank her for having the courage to remove it and for taking care of us all these years. I tell her that we have new tools and resources to use so she can rest for now. She will be safe as I use those new tools to take care of everyone. Then I release it into the ground to be transmuted into pure energy again.

Have you ever been in a conversation with someone, and all of the sudden you feel angry or frustrated? Take a moment to listen to what those voices are saying in your mind and where you feel that discomfort in your body. These are times when there is a belief you have that you aren't aware of that isn't actually true. Most of the time we jump right into the Drama Triangle when this happens, because that's become our way of dealing with things. We don't know we are doing it or that there is another way.

Most of us have not been given the tools and opportunities to really look into ourselves, into those dark places to find answers, and we really don't want to. It has become easier to deflect those feelings onto someone else. We have been taught to look outside ourselves for answers, but the real answers for us come from within. It can be difficult to sit with those voices in our heads telling us all those lies because we believe them to be true. It's when we can stop and look objectively that we can uncover the fear behind them.

I know this might sound very foreign, but in time it will become natural. These are clues for you to begin your introspection. We can all learn to listen to our voices. We just need a little guidance and maybe permission to start really questioning them. We can uncover what we believe about ourselves that is not true by listening to our thoughts. We just need to become aware that there is another way to think about things. While most of us think there is only one way, the right way to do something, or be something, that is simply not true. That is just those social constructs of our worth showing up as right or wrong, good or bad, to keep us stuck. We really don't know what we believe about ourselves and why. A little self-compassion, along with a little patience and understanding, will go a long way to uncovering those beliefs and becoming friends with those misunderstood voices from the past.

See it, Hear it, Live it

Let's connect to our hearts.

Take a moment to get settled... Close your eyes... Place your hand over your heart... feel your hand connect with your body and heart... relax... and breathe... breathe in...... and breathe out.... breathe in through the nose...

and breath out through the mouth, with a "ha" or sighing sound... continue this breath for as long as you like... when you are ready to end...simply come back to your normal breathing for a few moments... feel the connection of your hand on your heart, offer a moment of gratitude towards yourself... then take your hand from you heart and slowly open your eyes when you are ready.

CHAPTER 7

WHAT STOPS YOU IN YOUR TRACKS

I t's just before midnight as I lie down on the bed fully clothed. I know I will not sleep, yet I know I need rest. All of the night's events flash through my mind—the phone call asking me to come to the front door, Sgt. Harmon's death notification, heartfelt calls to family and friends to deliver the news. My husband is dead.

Darkness seems to take the life from the room. I am frozen with terror, and thoughts of being homeless flash through my mind. *I can't afford this house on my own. What am I going to do? I know, I can move the tenants out of the old house and move back in there. I can afford that if I am careful.*

That being solved, my thoughts return to Russ. *How will I afford a funeral? I know, I have the income tax check. That should be enough. I'm still dressed so let's go now to deposit the check.*

We are guided by so many unseen forces that we are totally unaware of in our lives. We spend most of our lives on autopilot and when something happens, we just react. As I look back on that night and all that unfolded, I now can see all the unseen forces that were in play that evening. The social constructs, my limiting beliefs, and my role in the Drama Triangle took over, as my body had its physical reaction to the fear that set in.

In the social constructs, women are taught they are the weaker sex and need to be protected by men. From a young age, women are programmed that becoming a wife and mother is our number one priority in life, so if you are not married or have children, then there must be something wrong with you. That need for a provider-protector is usually filled by our husband, so when Russ suddenly died, those unseen forces of the social constructs caused me to fear that I was weak and wasn't safe. I felt so unsafe that I had to get up and go to the bank and deposit a check in the middle of the night.

I also lost the title of wife. Now that he was dead, I was labeled a widow. That label left me feeling even more worthless and afraid. Wife was a greater label than widow, or simply Lesa, and I definitely did not want people feeling sorry for me or pitying me. I was so lost that night. *Who am I now? What is my worth now? I'm nothing.*

We all take on the roles and labels that others have given us without even knowing. The social constructs set up the foundation, and then we build on it unconsciously. Little things that seem harmless take on a life of their own, like taking your child's hand when you get out of the car or cross the street. We are unconsciously giving our children the label of not enough and instilling fear into them when we take their hand, telling them they might get run over by a car or abducted if they don't hold our hand.

You never know what is going to get linked together in a child's mind, and that is where all these things start. For me, food and TV are linked together to this day. Growing up, my family had a kitchen and living room that was one big room and it was the hub of the house. We all spent a lot of time there watching TV and cooking together, so now anytime I watch TV, I have to be eating even if I am not hungry.

There are other roles and labels that we wear that are just as unseen, such as the "twins' mother," "the golden child," or "Bill's wife." All of these leave us unaware of ourselves, who we really are. I don't think we even are given a chance to find out who we really are because we are always trying to be good enough, as defined by someone else, to have any value in the world.

When my husband was killed suddenly and I lost the role of wife and took on the label of widow, it was painful for me. I never knew who Lesa was, so I just took on the next label that the social constructs set out for me. I didn't like it, but I took it on. For me, widow seemed to invoke pity from others, and I didn't want that. I just wanted to be me, but I didn't realize that I didn't know myself and that I was really wanting that social construct back to give me more value in the world.

Unseen Beliefs Around Money

That long night, my limiting beliefs could have formed a crowd around me. Those unseen beliefs surrounding money showed up. I simply had to rush to the bank and deposit that check *right then* so I wouldn't be homeless. My scarcity belief caused such fear in me that I had to act on it by depositing a check that same night he was killed. I actually got up, got into the car, and drove to the bank.

I was taught that I always should be prepared for any situation and if I wasn't, I wasn't good enough. This night I certainly wasn't good enough.

I was taught that I should get a good-paying job with benefits, stay there thirty years and retire, but that was not what I had done. At the time of my husband's death, I was working at the Monte Carlo Casino in Las Vegas as a credit clerk. I basically looked into customers' financial backgrounds to determine if they were a good risk for credit or not. It was an eye-opening experience as I watched people chase the win. I worked in the industry for eight years and I saw people lose much more than they ever gained.

This job was not one that had much of a future for me. It certainly was not one of those jobs that paid well, had any advancement possibilities, or retirement, which I was taught to pursue. I did have those types of jobs in the past, but if I didn't feel happy at them, I would leave, taking the consequences for leaving that I believed would come.

I was taught that when you get one of those jobs, to hold on tight to it even if you are miserable, but I just couldn't do it. I realize now that I would leave those jobs, really looking to find me, only to find another one of those jobs. I thought I was seeking me, but I could never really seek like I needed to.

Who I truly am and was meant to be is not even in the realm of a job in my mind. I could never search in the right places because I never saw them. They were never open to me. The only thing I knew was getting that blue collar job with a retirement to take care of the family. That was the focus of a job, not self-satisfaction. You just had to keep your nose to the grindstone and work hard. Then you would be valuable to the boss.

In the fear that filled my mind, that left me only one choice: to be homeless, or maybe go back to the old house in the not-so-great neighborhood. Russ and I had recently moved into our new home, and it would take more than my income to afford it.

My mind was filled with thoughts such as, *Who do you think you are to have a dream home anyway? You don't deserve that dream house that you worked together to get. You didn't work hard enough to keep those things.*

For the first time in my life, I was living in a home in which I had decided what it would be. It was a brand-new build, and I watched it from the ground up. I was able to choose carpet that felt so soft it was like I was walking on clouds, and tile flooring that glistened like diamonds on the Sahara Desert. I created an oasis of peace and serenity using neutral wall colors, and the cabinetry throughout warmed the soul like a fire warms the body on a cold winter's night. It even had a two-car garage. But the true reason I loved it so much was the high ceilings. It felt expansive.

My previous house was block construction, with low ceilings and linoleum flooring. The laundry was done outside in a metal shed with the lawn equipment. The neighborhood was showing age and neglect. There were homes with windows boarded up, and cars that were no longer running sat in driveways. Many of the homes were missing roofing shingles and had overgrown bushes obstructing sidewalks and windows. The cinderblock always made me feel like I was in prison. It was really hard to put anything on the walls as I would have had to drill into the block walls. It never seemed like home to me.

I started beating myself up for all the bad choices I had made in life. *Who needs to be happy or fulfilled in their job?*

Nose to the grindstone—that's what matters. If you don't have a good-paying job that has good benefits and a retirement, then you must just be a slacker. No wonder no one wants to hire you. Now I had moved to the Victim role, adding fuel to the fire...*You better be glad for the little you do have, 'cause you will never have another nice thing in your life.*

In those times of fear, the unknown becomes a dark and dangerous place. Because of our negativity bias and our conditioned response, we fill the unknown with all the worst-case scenarios that we can think of. It becomes a perpetual cycle that we don't see and can't get ourselves out of. All the unseen forces conspire to hold us in a purgatory of our own making.

Most of us don't know why we do what we do or think what we think. We don't see the social construct that has defined what is right and wrong, what is valued and what is not. The social constructs have been set up to be infallible. It leaves us feeling that there is something wrong with us, and not the system, when we encounter difficulties in our lives.

We don't see the limiting beliefs that have developed over time because of those sacred people around us filling our minds with limitations. We don't see that as an adult we are still using those early learned manipulations from the Drama Triangle to get our needs met. It becomes a vicious cycle that consumes any joy or fulfillment in our lives.

When our mind perceives a threat, it sets to motion our fear response of fight-or-flight, and we have a physical response. The chemicals of adrenaline and cortisol are released in our bodies, giving us that boost of energy needed to fight or flee. Our culture has become one in which we tend to find constant stressors, which leads to our fear response always being turned on. We were not meant to live in a constant state of stress. Usually, the body's stress response system is self-limiting, and after the threat is gone, the body's hormones return to normal levels. The long-term activation of this stress response system upsets your body's processes and leaves you vulnerable to many health problems, such as:

- Depression
- Anxiety
- Weight gain
- Migraines
- Sleep problems
- Muscle tension and pain
- High blood pressure and stroke
- Heart disease and heart attack
- Memory loss and distraction

We have lived so long in this state of fatigue that it has become normal, and we don't think anything of it or even notice it anymore. It becomes a cultural norm within which we live. We fill ourselves with some caffeine and move on to the next thing we have to do.

We started being filled with these fears as children, and the fears grow as we become adults. I know parents are only trying to protect their children, but it somehow comes out differently than it is intended.

The Brownie Experience

When I was a young girl, I joined Brownies. I was so excited to attend my first meeting. I donned my brown dress and beanie and off we went. Mom dropped me off at the church where the meeting was being held. I walked into the social hall where the group of girls was gathered. Sitting down at the table, I saw a lot of new faces.

The group leader started the meeting by introducing herself and her assistant and then asked each of us to stand and introduce ourselves to the group. Because I lived in a rural area, we only had one Brownie troop, so all the girls came from neighboring communities. It was fun to meet all the new girls and get to know them.

After the introductions, the next agenda item was the rules of the troop and what adventures our troop would be involved in. The rules began with being polite, raising your hand to speak, much like all the things I had encountered in school. We made name tags, one to wear and one for our table and then it was time to go. We cleaned up and then waited.

I really paid attention to getting all the rules right. I made notes so I could remember. I was taught to respect authority and to always obey the rules. Following the rules was part of my identity of being a good girl. The troop leaders were all new authority figures to me, and I didn't want to disappoint them.

I didn't realize it at the time, but the meeting being held in a church added another dimension to the experience. My family never attended church. I had only been in a church a few times when a neighbor would take me to Vacation Bible School during the summer. I definitely got the message from our culture, though, that God held my eternity. I didn't want to offend him while I was at my Brownie meetings and end up going to hell.

At the next meeting, we started with the pledge of allegiance, and then got into our story and project of the day. During the story I got up to go to the bathroom. Just as I was about to leave the room, the troop leader stopped her story and addressed me.

"Lesa, where are you going?"

"I'm just going to the bathroom."

"Have you forgotten something? What did we learn from last week anytime we leave this room?"

"I don't remember."

"We never leave this room without telling an adult and taking another Brownie with us. You never know what might happen if you go out alone. You could get hurt or someone might take you away."

"I'm sorry, I will remember next time."

I felt embarrassed and confused. Why did I need someone to go to the bathroom with me? I never had before. Why would someone take me? How would I get hurt? I never went back to the Brownie meetings because of this incident.

Don't get me wrong. I am for teaching children of the dangers of things, but I know we can do better and teach them from a place of empowerment, not fear. We can teach them what to do to avoid situations or what to do if they find themselves in a situation. That empowers children—it doesn't leave them to fear everything.

These fears follow us into adulthood. Have you ever noticed when women go to the bathroom we tend go in pairs? A woman will usually ask another woman at the table if she needs to go to the bathroom if they are going. We rarely hear two men discussing at a table if they need to go to the bathroom or not. Men just get up and go. They were not socially constructed to see themselves as weak, as women have been socially constructed.

This is actually a perfect example of how a fear is buried beneath something that seems so ordinary. This is the great example of how these unseen forces move us about our lives. Women usually go in pairs when we are out in public. Women are taught from a young age that it is not safe to go anywhere alone, as even a trip to the bathroom has hidden dangers for us. The social construct that women are the weaker sex sets all this up. It has become ordinary—it's just what we do. We don't even see how it is based in fear.

There are so many ways that fear is instilled by the social constructs. We have so many authorities who tell us what to do and when to do it that we hardly even recognize it anymore because it has become so natural. We mostly just go throughout the day on autopilot, doing what we are supposed to do so we can get what we want.

We don't realize that we are being controlled by something that is bigger than us. Even if we see it, we think it's okay because what do we know. They are the authority and know better than we do.

I was in an IKEA a few months ago and had a very interesting experience with a friend. I don't usually go to IKEA because I don't like the energy in the store. For me, it feels very controlling and confining. As soon as you walk into the store, you are funneled into a maze. There are many displays lining a pathway through the store and there are arrows on the floor guiding your steps. The aisles are so narrow that you bump into others as you walk by.

We just ran in to pick up something, but they didn't have it, so we were going to just go out the way we came in and not go through the whole store like they have designed it. We got to the door that we thought we came in, but it said on the door, do not enter, emergency exit only, alarm will sound. My friend and I said simultaneously, how did we get the wrong door? We both stood there looking for a moment, but neither of us would take the chance and go through the door since there would be an alarm. It was just about that time an employee came by and walked right out the door. There was no alarm, and it wasn't even a fire door. We both were shocked and angry. I couldn't believe that a business would boldly lie to benefit themselves in such manner.

After leaving the store, my friend and I talked about our experiences for a moment. We both had experienced the same thing but to different ends. It seemed that we both got stopped in our tracks and fear set in when we read on the sign that an alarm would sound. Neither of us was willing to take that risk, even though we were both about ninety-nine percent sure that it was the door we came in. My next thought was that we could just walk through the store to get to the exit, but my friend was going to look for an employee to ask.

My kindergarten year in school was tough. I missed more than I was there. I had the measles, then the mumps on both sides at separate times, and I had a surgery to remove a tumor from my foot. Needless to say, I was not an easy student.

My teacher was frequently having to do extra work to keep me up to speed. When I came back from all that, I had to wear special shoes that were strapped, no shoestrings. In my class we had to take naps, which meant taking your shoes off. I guess I was slow putting them back on after our nap.

I'm not sure if my teacher's frustration was with me or someone else in the class but it got directed at me, and she yelled at me, "You are so dumb that you don't even know how to tie your shoes." From that day on I believed her, *I was dumb.* I didn't know how that comment would impact me the rest of my life.

I was taught to respect authority, especially teachers. For me, teachers were smart, so they certainly couldn't be wrong. In hiding those feelings of being dumb as a child, I found that doing for others seemed to get me recognition from adults. This relieved some of the feelings that I was dumb and worthless, but as a result, I took on the role from the Drama Triangle of Rescuer.

It made me feel worthwhile when someone gave me praise for what I could do. I never was really aware of how much of my value came from rescuing others. I never saw it in that light. I always loved helping others. Being extremely organized came naturally to me. Everyone loved me—friends, coworkers and supervisors alike—they all knew they could always count on me.

All of that doing for others and never taking care of myself eventually caught up with me. In looking back, the signs were subtle at first, but as the years progressed, the signs got bigger and bigger as eventually my gift became my curse.

I still wrestle with being dumb to this day. I am aware of this limiting belief, and yet it still can get the better of me some days. This pattern was started I believe in utero, as my mother was told how dumb she was for getting pregnant at fifteen. Being forced to leave high school as a result of being pregnant left her feeling dumb and worthless, a belief that was passed on to me.

All these fears that are instilled in us as children from the social constructs lead to our roles in the Drama Triangle as we search for our value. These fears set in motion the limitations we put on ourselves, and they most certainly cause us to run from the connection to our bodies. We try getting away from the pain through drugs, alcohol, food, sex—whatever we can find to relieve the suffering.

Most of our cultures around the world are built on a Dominator style of construction, being based on fear, power, and adherence to a strict hierarchy. These types of constructs can only leave participants feeling like *somewhere else is always better* and *more is all I'll ever need.* I believe that we are in the beginning stages of the process of moving from the Dominator style into a Co-operator, or Partnership, style of culture. The Co-operator culture is based on mutual respect and compassion. This style frees our innate capacities for joy and, as such, we can grow mentally, spiritually, and emotionally. This leaves room for our creativity, where power-with becomes empowerment, not power-over someone.

As we become aware of our fears and the patterns within ourselves, we can begin to alleviate the impact it has on our lives. We can slowly understand how it has crept into our lives, where it resides in our bodies, and work towards healing ourselves though self-love and compassion. As we change these patterns of fear, we can start to see infinite possibilities in the darkness of the unknown.

See it, Hear it, Live it

Let's connect with a body scan meditation:

Find yourself a quiet place to sit. Turn off your phone and dim the lights. Rest your hands loosely in your lap. Now close your eyes.

Take a long slow, deep breath in... hold it for a moment, and then slowly exhale. Just allow any tension to melt away as you gradually relax more and more deeply with each breath.

Take another long slow, deep breath in... hold it, and then exhale. Empty your lungs completely with your out-breath.

Take a third deep breath in. Take your time. Hold it for a moment, and then let it go. You can already feel yourself drifting into a state of deep relaxation.

Continue to breathe slowly and gently as you bring your awareness to the top of your head. Just sense or imagine a feeling of relaxation beginning to spread down from the top of your scalp... feel the muscles in your forehead and temples relax.

Allow your eye muscles to release. Let your cheeks and jaw soften and let go of all tension.

Now let this peaceful feeling flow down into your neck. Feel it loosening every muscle and every fiber.

With each breath you take, this relaxing feeling becomes deeper and warmer. It works its way deep into the muscles in your shoulders...soothing them...releasing them.

This peaceful feeling flows down from your shoulders and into your arms. It loosens the muscles in your upper arms...your forearms...your hands...relaxing and soothing...all the way to the tips of your fingers.

As your body relaxes, your mind relaxes, and your thoughts seem to become lighter. You are slipping further and further into a dreamlike state of stillness and relaxation.

Now, bring your awareness to your chest and your stomach. Feel how this area of your body gently rises and falls as you breathe. The peaceful sensation flows throughout this area of your body, soothing every muscle and relaxing every organ. You can feel it releasing every last molecule of tension.

Turn your attention to your upper back, and feel this relaxing sensation flow all the way down your spine. As it gradually works its way down your body, feel every muscle in your back relax and unwind.

Feel that your entire upper body has become loose, soft, and relaxed.

Sink into this serene sensation. Relax more and more deeply with each breath.

Now feel your hips relax as the peaceful feeling starts to work its way through your lower body. Relax your buttocks...the backs of your thighs...the front of your thighs. Feel all these large, strong muscle groups becoming looser and more relaxed with each passing moment.

Soothing feelings of relaxation flow down through your knees, and into your calves. Your ankles relax. Now your feet relax. Allow your entire lower body to relax completely and allow any remaining tension from anywhere in your body to flow out through the tips of your toes.

You are comfortable, peaceful, and relaxed. Sit like this for a few more moments, taking in a few deep breaths. When you're ready, open your eyes.

CHAPTER 8

FEEL AND BE SEEN

I've been wanting a getaway for months now, but I keep putting it off for a better time. A friend reminds me that there will never be that perfect time and to just make the plans. I decide I want to go to Sedona, Arizona. I love the energy there. It's where I go alone when I need to rejuvenate. I make a reservation at my favorite hotel and set up an afternoon with a holistic healer. I love trying new things when I go there.

As the time nears for my trip, I see that there is going to be a winter storm on the day I am to drive to Sedona. I weigh the pros and cons of going and proceed with my plans. I've driven in snow before; I'll travel in the daytime, and it's only four and a half hours to Sedona from Las Vegas.

I head out for Sedona early in the morning. The sun is shining in Las Vegas, and I'm feeling great. I'm taking my typical route, traveling US-93S, I-40E and State Route 89A. I get into Kingman, Arizona, and make my way onto I-40E. This is the part of the trip that takes me into the higher elevations, so this is where the snow will be.

A blanket of snow stretches across these higher elevations, but the roads are clear and I'm making great time. All of the sudden, I see above me a lighted road sign that tells me there is an accident ten miles ahead. I drive a few more miles as the traffic slows and comes to a complete stop.

It's still early so I'm not sweating this delay. After sitting in the car for an hour, I get out to stretch my legs. As I'm walking around my car, a semi-driver gets my attention, telling me that the accident ahead involves thirteen vehicles including four big rigs, so it will be some time before the highway is reopened. Somehow, I remain optimistic.

It's been two hours now and I'm getting out of the car to stretch my legs again. I can feel the anxiety and tension building in my body as the delay lingers on. I'm not panicked yet, but my mind is telling me, *Let's get going. You know there is a winter storm coming and you don't want to be driving at night.*

Hour after hour passes, and snow starts falling intermittently. Each time I get out of the car to stretch, I can feel the ice building beneath my feet as I struggle to keep my balance. It's been almost six hours now, darkness is quickly approaching, and the temperature is dropping. Snow is falling steadily now.

In my mind, I hear the distant chatter of voices telling me, *Whose idea was this to take a trip during a winter snow warning? I told you so. It's going to be dark, and the roads are going to be dangerous now, what were you thinking? You don't really need to take a trip anyway. What have you done to deserve a vacation anyway?* I feel the tension building in my body and the anxiety growing in my mind, but I keep telling myself everything will be fine. *It's not the first time you have been to Sedona and although it's been a while since you have driven in snow, you have done it before so don't worry.* As more tension builds in my body and fear starts to set in, I tell myself when the accident clears, I'll just turn around and go home. That's the safest thing to do. But now I am already closer to Sedona than I am to home. I will have to drive back through the worst area again, and that doesn't make sense to do.

Finally, we slowly start moving after six hours of sitting and waiting on the interstate. Darkness is upon us and the snow is now falling heavily, but I am glad to just be moving. I am panicked, but managing. I keep telling myself *just drive slowly, take your time, you are okay.* As time wears on, the traffic starts moving faster; I can feel more and more tension building in my body, as I grip the wheel tighter.

Finally, I see the sign for Sedona. I turn off I-40 onto State Route 89A. It is dark, and I am alone. I'm thinking, *Wait for someone to follow.* I know there are others going to Sedona.

I negotiate the exit and turn off onto State Route 89A, the start of the canyon. *OMG, the snow is falling so hard, and it is about a foot deep!!!* I keep driving but now I am in full meltdown mode, panicked to the point I'm not thinking straight. My breathing has become rapid and shallow, and I can hear my heart pounding.

I can't see the road for all the fallen snow. There are no tire tracks, and the snow is falling so hard that the windshield wipers do nothing. I drive a little further, then I see it, ROAD CLOSED THRU THE CANYON. I am in major meltdown now! Now what, follow the detour—what detour? I can't even see my hand in front of my face, it's so dark. I hope for a connection on my phone for directions.

A surreal feeling comes over me as I stop the car in the middle of the road. It's beautiful. A blanket of white. Trees heavy with snow on their branches. A sense of peace and quiet comes over me as I watch the big flakes of falling snow. It's a winter wonderland.

As I come back from this moment, I realize I have no idea where I'm going, it's dark, and the roads are treacherous. I feel a terror come over me, I reach for my cellphone, praying for a connection. Ah, there it is, one tiny bar, I enter the address of the hotel, manage to turn around, and head back to the interstate.

It's so dark, the snow is falling heavily, and my hands grip the steering wheel tightly as I get on the interstate. As I look up ahead of me, I see two snowplows, so I fall in behind them. I am so thankful and feel safe for a moment, but that feeling doesn't last long.

The voices return again, *You're going too fast! You can't see the road, and there is a sheet of ice covering it! You're going to die on this road! Why did you even try driving Sedona knowing there was a winter snow warning? You are such a fool!* I look for a place to get off the road, but there is none. I look for a motel to stop at for the night, but there is none. I must keep moving with every part of my being telling me to stop.

I try to keep the voices in my head at bay as they tell me I'm in danger. They are winning, though. My body is so tense, and now the adrenaline and cortisol are on full flow. Even though I couldn't ask for anything more than to be following two snowplows, those voices are powerful, and I can't shake the feeling of fear.

All of the sudden the two snowplows turn off the interstate. Tears start welling up in my eyes as I've lost my only protection. Now what? I slow down and keep driving.

I'm so frightened that I'm numb. My hands are fatigued from gripping the steering wheel, and I am exhausted. I feel like every muscle of my body has been running for twenty-six miles, a full marathon.

Now I really have to talk to myself. I just keep telling myself that I am safe. I can handle this. I just keep repeating those words out loud until I feel a little give in my body. The roads are starting to have less snow on them, and I can see some lights in the distance. Surely that is Sedona.

There it is, Exit 179 N Sedona, one mile. Such a relief comes over my body. I can feel the tension draining from me, and now I feel extremely fatigued. I make the turn off I-17 onto Hwy 179 through Oak Creek Canyon and drive the 30 miles to the hotel. It's 11:30 p.m. as I drive into the hotel parking lot and pull into my parking space under the flickering of the streetlamp. I made it.

The Truth Center

As a culture we have become disconnected from our bodies. For most of us listening to our bodies is a foreign idea. All we know is when something hurts, we relieve it with a pill, potion, or salve.

When we feel an emotion, not only do our minds react, so do our bodies. Our body holds our emotional experiences like memories. For instance, sadness, grief, and loss are held in our lungs, fear is held in our kidneys, worry is held in our spleen, anger in our liver, and depression and restlessness are held in our heart. When our bodies feel, and our minds don't like what it sees, we use a coping mechanism to bypass those feelings. These coping mechanisms take many forms such as drugs, alcohol, food, TV, and sex. It feels better to use these coping mechanisms than to really understand what is going on. It has become the norm to disconnect from our bodies, so much so that we don't even realize that we are doing it.

The trip I took to Sedona is a perfect example of the mind-body connection. I was never really in danger, but my fears set in, and my body went into the fight-or-flight response. I responded by gripping the wheel tighter and my breathing became faster and shallower.

If I had only one of those fears that came into my reality, I might have been able to slowly regain my composure, but I had too many unknowns that overpowered anything that my rational mind could pose to me. As more of my voices showed up, greater fear set in, and I was literally flooded with cortisol and adrenaline. It just kept flooding in because I was sure that something bad was going to happen. I didn't know where I was going. I was lost and I knew that I was no match for mother nature. I was at her mercy. The fact that it was dark now was a huge factor as well. The voices of fearing the dark showed up, as well as the voices of a women shouldn't be traveling alone because something might happen to her.

When we come up against an unknown, fear sets in, and we go back to our programming. Those voices in our heads are that programming. My programming taught me to fear the dark and that women have a good chance of being hurt if they travel alone.

Growing up, I would hear adults saying that only bad people are out at night or watch out when you go out at night because someone will jump out from the dark and hurt you. I definitely got the cultural message that women are weak, and not to do anything alone. In doing so, you were just asking for trouble.

Just knowing that none of that is true is not enough to overcome these programs. We must create space for ourselves. The space for us to change. The space I'm talking about is that between the stimulus of an event and our response to it.

There are many ways to change our responses, and one of them is breathing. My surreal moment in the snowstorm was actually space, but I didn't recognize it at the time. When I realized that I would need to turn around and find another way to Sedona, I took a deep breath to gear up for a change. That breath created space for me to do something different. Even though it was short-lived, I could see the beauty of the falling snow and hear the peace that surrounded me.

There are many ways to create space for our minds to deal with those voices. Here are a few more ideas for you to consider.

- Journaling
- Meditation
- Decluttering
- Talking with a friend
- Getting out in nature
- Limiting social media
- Playing—Find something you love and do it.

Creating this space will take practice, so be kind to yourself in the process. Try out different ways for different situations. Finding your patterns will go a long way in helping you find what works to reprogram them. Take it one step at a time. This programming didn't happen overnight, and it will take some time to overcome it.

The cultural norm in dealing with the fear of these unseen forces has become for us to busy ourselves so we don't have to think about it. No one wants to admit they are afraid, and for the most part we don't even know we are. It has become so ingrained that it has become just what you do.

The parent-child conditioning starts early. Most of us have been taught that bad things happen in the dark and only those people who are up to no good are out at night. Our parents tell us not to stay out late because something bad will happen to us, so be home early.

Cultural conditioning sets in as well. Most of us have been taught that women are the weaker sex and need someone strong—a man—to protect them. We all have visceral responses to these unseen forces, but we rarely recognize them.

While we all deal with stress differently, becoming busy seems to be a go-to for a lot of us. This is how most of us go about our day, acting on some sort of stress response, and we don't even know it. It has become a part of our culture. Everyone is always running late... Everyone has overextended themselves... Everyone has to get the kids to school... Everyone has to fight the traffic getting to work... It's become a way of life and for some it's become where they get a large part of their value in the world. If I have all these things to do, I must be someone, right? We do not value our bodies until we have to, and by that time it's usually too late—the damage has already been done. When we don't listen to those nagging aches and pains, they become bigger. Our bodies have our lives stored in them. That story can be a guide for us if we can slow down long enough to listen.

Because we don't place much value on listening to our bodies, we all have gotten out of the practice of hearing it. Our bodies literally have to scream at us to be heard. When we can slow down and sit with the discomfort for a moment, listening to its message, we can start on the path to healing our bodies and our minds.

I didn't listen to my body until I was forced. Remember, I am a huge Rescuer. I take on everyone's burdens, so I feel the weight of the world on my shoulders. I do everything for everyone, and nothing for myself. I am one of those people that think, as the flight attendant is giving the preflight safety instructions, that I can put everyone's masks on before my own, including the flight crew, and land the plane if needed, and I will be fine.

When we don't pay attention in our lives, the lessons get bigger, and more is required to negotiate them. I hadn't been listening, my sound level was set to mute, so the universe ramped up the volume. I had two people in my life that I dearly loved, so the universe decided to use them for me to rescue and I did.

I was so stressed but I couldn't see what I was doing, and I didn't know how to get out of the situation and maintain the relationships. They had become so dependent on me. I didn't know that my value in most of my relationships was in what I could do for others. I didn't know that I had the belief that if I stopped doing for them, they wouldn't need me, love me, or want me in their lives.

My stress started to physically manifest itself in bigger ways, as the more subtle body signals of headaches, irritability, and exhaustion weren't getting my attention. I started falling down a few times, bumping my head, twisting my ankle. Then I got into a few accidents, one fracturing my toe. I slowed down a little, but I still wasn't listening to my body.

It took the excruciating pain of a pinched nerve for me to be stopped in my tracks and really think about what was going on. It was September 2019, and I had just returned from a trip to Texas to see my family. The next morning, I woke up with this pain from another world in my back that ran down my leg. The pain was nothing that I have ever felt before and hope never to feel again. Nothing helped to relieve it. I suffered for ten days thinking that it would just go away. I ended up going to the doctor for an injection to relieve the pain before I could even start really understanding the pain.

During those ten days I could only walk around, pacing at night for the pain to be tolerable. I never sat down as it was excruciating. I cried most of the night as the pain was so intense. Tears would just roll down my face.

This was my wakeup call. Only once I really started to listen to the pain did I learn what it was trying to tell me. All the weight I had physically gained plus the weight of taking on others' burdens was too much for me. I had to learn that everything in the world was not my responsibility to resolve. I didn't even know that's how I was really thinking. I had no idea that my gift had become my curse and it was killing me slowly.

My gifts of organization, foresight, and connection ended up being my biggest stressors. I'm an awesome organizer, and I easily see ahead so I'm ready always prepared for the next step. I also have an exceptional ability to see the greatness in others, and to connect on a deep level. So, if you are in my life, we have a deep soul connection, and I'm always seeing ways to make your life easier. These are awesome gifts to go through life with, yet they became my downfall. I didn't know that I was using them for love and approval.

One morning in a yoga class, as I was struggling with the tree pose, the instructor told us that we should be striving for balance in our lives. What is balance anyway? I never understood that until recently.

- Balance is the connection with others in harmony with the connection to self.
- Balance is being content where you are.
- Balance is the ability to be in the present moment.

We are taught to look for something outside of ourselves to make us feel good and to be valued. Yes, we need connection with others, but somehow what we call connection now is more like an unhealthy attachment. We need that person to make us feel good about ourselves, putting an unseen burden on the relationship.

We need balance in our lives, but our culture leaves us believing that someplace else is always better and more is all we will ever need, so we keep searching for that one fix to our problems.

Balance looks and feels like something we have never experienced, so do we want it? The first time I experienced it, I felt like I had all of a sudden become a sociopath. As I started to move away from the extreme, it felt so unfamiliar. My end of the extreme was doing everything for everyone that asked. I didn't even realize that I was slowly changing at the time, but when my best friend asked me to take care of her dog for two weeks and I said no, I knew something was going on because I didn't have the same typical feelings of guilt I would have in the past.

Those feelings of guilt had left me, but now I felt that I was no longer a caring and compassionate person. I felt like I was bad because I didn't care about other people any longer. Doing for others had become my connection to them, so when I stopped doing it, I felt numb.

It was so unsettling that I actually asked my friends if they noticed a difference in me. They told me I seemed more grounded, self-confident, and loving. They said they felt more connected to me.

Wow, what was happening? The more I stopped rescuing, the more I actually got what I thought the rescuing was giving me—a deep, soul level connection with others. I used rescuing to get people to need me, love me, and want me in their lives, to feel worthy. I didn't even realize what I was really wanting: connection, to be seen and heard for who I am, to be loved and appreciated for just being.

As I moved away from rescuing, I could be seen more for something outside of that and I could see others from another perspective as well. As I began to have more time for myself, I started to get to know myself and actually started to love who I was. My love for myself opened up another part of me that had been dormant for a long time. I was filled with love and joy for life, and those near me felt it.

Looking to Nature for Balance

I look at balance in nature, and it looks nothing like what we strive for in life. Nature is full of connection and balance, but most of it looks so harsh that we have to turn away from it. I look at how fire brings new growth and birth to the earth, but all we see is destruction. In order for something new to come into our lives we have to let go of something, but we want to hold onto everything because most of us live in a world of scarcity. We can only see what we will lose but not what we can gain.

When we are in balance, we are in the present moment. For most of us, this is an unfamiliar place, as we spend most of our time in the past or the future. We spend a lot of time looking for something to fear without even realizing it. The unknown is a very scary place because we fill it with our doubts and insecurities as our culture has taught us. It doesn't have to be that way. The unknown could just as easily be filled with infinite possibilities if we think it is. What we think is our truth.

That surreal moment on the trip to Sedona, when I was so frightened, was actually me being connected to the present moment. I had gotten myself to such a panicked state that I took a deep breath, and that connected me to my body, giving it some space, connecting me to my rational mind for a moment. I was able to feel safe and see the beauty in the moment.

Being out of balance has become the norm of our culture. A disconnection from ourselves has led to a disconnection from others and that frightens us. That causes us to hold on so tightly to what little we feel we have, that we actually end up killing it.

We can only be connected to others as much as we are connected to ourselves. Knowing and understanding ourselves is the key to connecting to others. We have been fooled into thinking that doing for ourselves is being selfish, but it is the only way forward. We cannot connect to ourselves if we don't take the time for self-care, to know what makes us who we are.

There are so many unseen forces that are keeping us from connecting to ourselves. We have been taught what to want and how to think. It's time that we stop and really try on all these things to see who we truly are.

I know as adults we are supposed to know all this, and it can be difficult to go back and do things that our culture says we should have done as a child. We never really had the chance to search as a child, so we have to do it now. We just believe we did because that is what we are told. As a child, we just did what our parents told us, as we really had limited control over our own lives. We never had the opportunity to really try things on to see if they really fit us.

Do as You're Told

It seems so often that we must have a big event in our lives to get us to move forward. We almost have to be forced to do something we know we need to do, but it's outside of our comfort zone. Maybe we don't even know we need something, but those big life changes give us the opportunity to move forward.

After the death of my husband, I really started trying things on and I got a lot of grief over it. A good friend of the family told me that since Russ's death I had been wandering. I was so upset that I didn't talk to her for months. At the time, it made me feel like there was something wrong with me because I didn't know, and as an adult, I should have. Now I can embrace my wandering and see it as something positive, a sign of growth in my life.

The year of this writing is 2022, marking twenty-four years since Russ's death. Looking back on my life, I can see that I went from one role to the next role—daughter to my mother, wife to my husband, then widow after his death. I never searched for who Lesa was. I was just always fitting into the next role, the right thing on the path set before me.

Wandering, in my family, was something you didn't do. You had a set direction and you followed it no matter what. After Russ's death, I was lost. I didn't know who I was because I didn't know Lesa. I did have to wander to find her, and it was uncomfortable for me. I had to renegotiate long-held beliefs about being a woman, in the role of wife, and now the role of widow.

It was an awkward time for me. I felt comfortable and safe as wife but now being alone, especially as a widow, I felt vulnerable and uncertain. As I searched for Lesa, she slowly appeared before me, and I found that I didn't need so many of those social constructs for my value. I was good enough just being Lesa.

Sometimes it takes such a shock to get us out of autopilot, to start to see things in a different light. We don't have to wait for such huge events to force us to do so—we just need to slow down and take a look at all the unseen forces that are limiting our lives and make small changes to end up in a totally different direction.

See It, Hear It, Live It

Let's connect with a mind-body visualization.

For this visualization sit down and get into a comfortable position. Relax and take a few deep breaths.

Imagine that you're in your kitchen, standing in front of a counter, and on the counter, there is a cutting board, a lemon, and a knife.

1. Pick up the lemon, walk over to the sink, turn on the water, and wash the lemon.

2. The water is cool as you feel it against your hand. Turn the water off, take a paper towel, dry the lemon; really feel the towel in your hand, feel the lemon, and then walk back to the cutting board on the counter.

3. Place the lemon on the cutting board, keeping one hand on the lemon. Pick up the knife in your other hand.

4. Feel the weight of the knife in your hand. It's a little heavy because it's a hefty knife. Now keeping one hand on the lemon, take your knife and slice the lemon in half.

5. When you slice through that lemon, a little bit of lemon juice squirts out and you feel it on your hand, and it is cold.

6. Now you've got half of the lemon in one hand. I want you to put that half down on the counter on top of the cutting board and I want you to cut through it again.

7. A little more lemon juice squirts out and now you've got a wedge of lemon. Put your knife down on the counter, take the wedge of lemon, and put it up just under your nose and take a deep breath in.

8. Now take a bite out of that lemon—did anything happen, did your mouth water or did it pucker up?

I'm sure you had an experience like so many people if your mouth watered or you puckered up just thinking about that lemon. You just had a mind-body response.

CHAPTER 9

THE ROAD TO YOUR SUCCESS

By now you have an understanding about the unseen forces that have been holding you back from leading the fulfilling life you want. You are slowly identifying the social constructs that have been the foundation of your life, and you have been sifting through them to see what fits you. You are reframing those limiting beliefs that you have held you in their grip for so long, gaining a sense of empowerment. You are challenging those fears that would stop you in your tracks in the past, and you are seeing the infinite possibilities as you walk into the darkness of the unknown with courage.

You have experienced your innate worth, and no longer seek it from an external source, so those voices in your mind have less power over you. As you are identifying your roles in the Drama Triangle and are shifting them, you are creating space for that mind body connection that leads to well-being. You are truly becoming who you were meant to be and building a life that supports it.

You will know that you have mastered these unseen forces when you notice that you are making different choices in response to your experiences in life. You will be able to feel in the moment when these unseen forces arise as you have developed your mind-body connection, giving you the ability for understanding and avoiding so much dysfunction. There will be a sense of lightness in your body and life. You will notice that you see things from a totally different perspective. You will feel thrilled to be you and to be alive.

Being able to know when you have fallen back into old patterns or meeting a new challenge will be key to moving forward. So how do you know when you're moving forward and not just stuck in the same old patterns? Does your life look different? Are you responding differently to situations? Are you starting to be able to notice physical responses in real time to situations? Do you have that moment of breathing space in the heat of an argument? These are all signs of progress. If you're not seeing any changes in your life and you don't find yourself questioning things, you are likely in your old patterns. Don't get discouraged. The fact that you can see that is actually progress, too.

Self-exploration is a lifelong process. It seems as if we are looking for that one thing that will turn the tide in our lives. Somehow, we have been led to think that one person can help us find the way. In a sense, that is true, but that one person is us, not someone else. There is no one magic formula that cures all our ills. It really does "take a village." We must decipher and sift through all that comes into our lives, becoming our own alchemist of sorts, melding our own gold.

There will be times that you think you want to turn back to the way things used to be, because the lessons seem never ending, and you just want a break. You will most certainly be drawn back in by all these unseen forces, and you will feel like you haven't learned a thing along the way. You will become fatigued and question yourself, is it worth it? Yes, it is...be patient and kind with yourself along the way.

You will get frustrated with yourself when you see another way to react in situations, but still act in the old ways. It will take time to rewire all those circuits from the old patterning. At first you won't even see your old programming in action until the moment has passed, when you are trying to figure out what just happened. In time, you will be able to feel the trigger in the moment and react in a way that is empowering and not from the Drama Triangle. Trust the process. It will get easier, I promise.

There will be times as you are growing and changing that you don't seem to know yourself any longer. You will look in the mirror and ask, who is this person? I don't know you. There will be people in your life that notice the changes too, and they will start to question you. As a result, you will start to question yourself if this is right. It is. It just feels so unfamiliar to you because it is. It will feel like your whole world is falling apart, because it is... You are rebuilding a totally new life for yourself so of course it will look and feel different.

There will not be many, if any, people in your life that want to see your growth. They want to keep the relationship with you that works for them. Don't get caught up in their drama.

As you start seeing your relationships changing, it will feel very unsettling. Don't get thrown off balance by it.

You may feel alone as you watch people fade from your life. It is natural that people come and go from our lives.

This time it will feel different because you are different. We have to clear out the old to receive the new. Be gentle with yourself during this time. Waiting for the new, especially when you feel alone, can seem like an eternity, or that it will never happen. Trust yourself, it will come.

Like anything else in life, practice makes perfect. This new way of being and thinking is no different. Just as you would work out in a gym, you will need to have a daily practice in place for this new way of being. It may sound a little odd, and you may be thinking I don't need to practice living your own life. These are all new concepts, and they are the total antithesis to the way you have been living, so you will need something to guide you until it becomes part of you.

These are the things that I started doing every day that really seemed to make a difference for me. I have developed them into the daily practice of See it, Hear it, Live it. They have taken different shapes and forms over the years, but I do them every day. Use them to develop your own practice, make it your own, and do what feels right for you.

- Meditation
- Nature
- Mindfulness
- Gratitude

These four areas of the See it, Hear it, Live it daily practice will help you to slow down, and build the mind-body connection, giving you a zeal for life. The practice of mindfulness and meditation helps you to slow down and to be in the present moment. This helps the mind-body connection where you can recognize and accept your thoughts, feelings, and sensations without judgments. A practice of mindful meditation gives you the opportunity to listen to your body, mind, and surroundings.

The act of being in nature as you do this practice gives an amplification of sorts as nature is a great healer. According to *Psychology Today*, studies have shown nature to be the purest pathway to inner peace, as it reenergizes you and restores your psyche. Even just being shown pictures of nature lights up the areas of the brain that are linked to love and empathy.

Being in nature grounds you and allows you to have the mental space for thinking differently, thus seeing things in a new way. This is why doctors and therapists recommend taking a walk or getting exercise outdoors for depression. It elevates our mood. It also connects us to our bodies by feeling the sun on our skin, the breeze across our face, the earth under our feet, and the smells passing our nose.

A practice of mindfulness brings you into the present moment. What is usually causing our struggle is something from our past or the future that we can't change or that we are worried about happening. Being in just this moment, we have access to our body-mind connection, and we can experience the peace of being right here right now. Being in this one moment is doable, and it gives us a foundation to build on. When we look at all the things we have to do or be, we can get overwhelmed. Practicing mindfulness gives us a success to build on.

Mindfulness is to be in the now, to take up all the space in the present moment, and being seen and heard. Being fully present in the moment is not something most of us practice daily. Most of us spend the greatest amount of our time in the past or the future, worrying about something that has already happened or might happen. Being in the present moment being able to make peace with who and where we are, right now in this very moment, is where the magic can happen. It's where we can have the biggest impact in our lives, to be fully present in this moment.

The practice of gratitude brings joy into our lives. David Steindl-Rast said, "It's not joy that makes us grateful; it's gratitude that makes us joyful." The practice of gratitude is not just, yeah, I'm thankful for and then naming something. It needs to be something you do every day and it needs to be tangible. For it to truly be gratitude, you need to feel it in your body. When we practice gratitude, we are building up a muscle that we are not used to using much, so it does take practice. Gratitude boosts the neurotransmitter serotonin which causes our brain to produce dopamine, our brain's pleasure chemical. We need to feel gratitude like when we were children on Christmas morning anticipating opening our gifts. Remember that feeling? That's the body-mind connection you are looking for.

How do we get there? Little steps, with things like writing in a journal, or at a certain time each day saying one thing you are grateful for out loud. I started doing a small act of kindness each day by just smiling at people, something that we think of as so small as not to matter much. The act of smiling is actually very beneficial to us as well. When we smile, it starts a chain reaction of chemical release in our bodies. Among those chemicals are dopamine and serotonin, which are "feel good" chemicals.

It is important for you to be open and explore in this process. You don't know what you don't know about yourself, but with each step you are moving toward your authentic self. There are things that you are still carrying around that you are not aware of. Here is an example of what I am talking about. I was eating lunch in a restaurant the other day, and as the server was giving me my check, the young man that was sitting a couple seats away from me asked if he could buy my lunch for me. My immediate reaction was *no, and hell no. What do you want from me? I don't want to owe you anything. I'm not worthy.* I could feel that my body wanted to flee. Where had all this fear come from?

I was totally surprised by my response to his question. As all this internal dialogue and struggle was going on, I did manage to gain my composure and said yes to the offer, and I thanked the young man for being so kind. The experience was very revealing and showed me yet another level of fear that is keeping me from receiving. This fear keeps me held captive and keeps me from my true self. Most importantly it keeps me from receiving all the universe has for me, and dims my light.

Be curious. Don't make assumptions on what you will like or not like. Try everything on again. I would have never imagined my morning routine now. I get up at 3 A.M. and do a walking meditation of sorts under the stars. I love it! I have been doing it for a few years now.

As I walk the unpaved trail, I'm soaking in the nature all around me. It looks and feels very different in the dark. I am also practicing mindfulness as I am present in the moment. I find that I am able to stay more in the present when I'm in nature. I don't think we spend enough time in the moment. We are usually either in the future or the past worrying.

My gratitude ritual has been an unexpected source of empowerment for me. As I walk, I say aloud all the things I am grateful for, and it is an amazing experience. It is more than just reciting affirmations; you must actually feel the gratitude in your body. You need to feel it as if you already possess it. In the beginning you may not feel everything you are grateful for, but just keep believing.

Here are a few things that I have daily reminders set for in my phone, and I always include in my gratitude for the day...

- I am grateful for trusting the process.
- I am grateful that infinite possibilities lie within the darkness of the unknown.
- I am grateful that even when I can't see a way there is always a way.
- I am grateful for all the people from around the world who are seeking me out for my wisdom and healing abilities.
- I am grateful for my naturally lean, strong, healthy, beautiful, youthful body.
- I am grateful for the overflowing abundance of success in my life.
- I am grateful for being in the right place at the right time.
- I am grateful I belong.

These are just a few, but they give you an idea of where to start. I started with the things that I really wanted to become more at one with. Find what works for you and build on it.

There are many forms of meditation, so I suggest you try different styles to see what you like. You will find that there are days that you feel like doing a certain kind. In the beginning I did mostly guided ones, but even then, there are so many kinds of guided meditations. I also used sound therapy as a meditation. I played my gong and just let the vibrations wash over me. You can find some good sound baths online. Be creative with your meditation; staring into the flame of a candle can be meditative. Start with anything that you are drawn to and go from there.

Getting out into nature is great for our overall wellbeing. It helps with the body mind connection. It can help us to unplug and slow down. Being outdoors is a great mood booster. Find something you enjoy doing outside, maybe hiking, kayaking, fishing, birdwatching, cycling, or roller skating. Whatever it is, enjoy it. Slow down and be present, because you are so worth it.

Practicing mindfulness is really just practicing being in the present moment. Meditation, yoga, and breathing exercises are good ways to practice. Remember to be kind, patient, and non-judgmental with yourself as you start this practice. I don't think we realize how little we are really in the present moment.

Practicing gratitude can be in any form you choose. I started off with just saying to myself three things before I went to bed that I was grateful for each night. I've done gratitude journals where I wrote down ten things each day that I was grateful for. Find what works for you. The key is to do it daily and to really feel it. Feeling it in your body is the key to manifesting it, because when you can feel it, you believe it.

Be patient with yourself. You may have been doing these practices for years and it hasn't made a difference. The key to it all is to be in the now, this present moment. To take up all the space in this moment. It's a place that we are unfamiliar with, so it will take some time and practice. Start with connecting to your breath, for it is the quickest way to our mind-body connection. It's the easiest way for us to come into our bodies.

Be sure you are connecting to your breath in your body, not your mind. Put your hand over your heart and feel that area. Make sure you feel a shift, or drop, into your body. This is most likely why it hasn't worked for you in the past—you were still in your head. When you do this, you will see how disconnected from yourself you are. Slowly, with practice, you will uncover your inner wisdom. As you connect to your inner world, your outer world will naturally align, and you will find yourself seen and heard in the world.

My hope for you is to build that life you could have never imagined. To find that one-of-a kind person within yourself that is waiting to shine, living each day with love and excitement to be alive. Go within yourself to find your answers. Remember, "It's never too late to give up what you are doing and start doing what you realize you love."—Hans Rosling.

See it, Hear it, Live it

Let's connect with a laughter meditation...

Let's start by standing with your feet hip-width apart and stretch your arms over head, then bend over as far as comfortable, just dangle your arms and sway. Remember to breathe and just relax. When you feel ready, return to a standing position for a few moments.

Now find yourself a comfortable sitting or standing position. Start by bringing a smile to your face and then begin to laugh without too much effort. Now move to deep belly laughs... Try different types of laughs to inspire your true laugh to come through. Do this for three to five minutes. Don't worry if at first it feels forced. Your authentic laughter will show up.

Now let's sit or lie on the floor, listening in silence, just listening for what comes up. Are thoughts coming up? How does your body feel? What emotions do you feel? Take some time and journal what comes up for you or what realizations have been revealed.

ACKNOWLEDGMENTS

I want to thank Betty Turnbull, Wally Turnbull, Jori Hanna, and Erica Zaborac of Torchflame Books for all their support and guidance in publishing my first book. I am grateful for the opportunity to work with such a wonderful publishing company.

A big thank you to Reid Tracy, of Hay House, and Kelly Notaras, of KN Literary Arts, for holding their online writers' workshop. I would not have written this book without attending your workshop. I appreciate the love of writing that you both have.

Thank you to Donna Galassi, of KN Literary Arts, for guiding me to the right editor for this project.

My coaching editor, Carolyn Flynn, of SoulFire Studios, I can't thank you enough for all your help. Your guidance during the process was invaluable; *Seen And Heard* would not have been birthed into the world without your love and support.

My family and friends were a huge support network; they were always there when I needed a word of encouragement. Mom, Thank you for believing in me and supporting me in sharing our story. Paula, I am so grateful for our friendship. You are my biggest cheerleader. Andrew, Thank you for all the "juicing;" without it, I would not have the material foundation of *Seen And Heard*. Suzanne, Thank you for showing me a world I would have never known. Shu, Thank you for always getting me back on track when I would get distracted. I love you all and am grateful for you in my life.

Russ, you have been gone for twenty-four years, not a day goes by that I don't miss you. I'm so thankful for our life together; you live on through me.

I am so grateful to K-pop artists Henry Lau, and Lay Zhang. Your creativity and talent are inspiring; you made me look deeper into myself and see the beauty within me. Your courage to be you, and do your thing, gave me the confidence to shine my light brighter.

A book is only the beginning for a writer, a reader completes it, and you are an example of this. Thank you so much taking the time to read my book, I am truly grateful. My hope is that it brought you what you were looking for. Please feel free to reach out to me, I would love to hear from you.

ABOUT THE AUTHOR

Lesa Peterson grew up in a rural farming community south of Chicago, Il, and now lives in Las Vegas, NV. She became a widow in her early thirties, which sent her on a journey spanning twenty years, leading to the culmination of this work. She has integrated the well-being of body, mind, and spirit into a beautiful tapestry that leads to inner wisdom.

Connect with Lesa:

lesapeterson.com
lesa@lesapeterson.com
Facebook: lesa.peterson.39
Instagram: lesalynnpeterson
youtube: @lesapeterson134

CPSIA information can be obtained
at www.ICGtesting.com
Printed in the USA
BVHW041508020723
666648BV00002B/60

9 781611 535198